Down to Earth

Down to Earth

Christian Hope and Climate Change

Richard A. Floyd

CASCADE *Books* • Eugene, Oregon

DOWN TO EARTH
Christian Hope and Climate Change

Copyright © 2015 Richard A. Floyd. All rights reserved. Except for brief quotations in critical publications or reviews, no part of this book may be reproduced in any manner without prior written permission from the publisher. Write: Permissions, Wipf and Stock Publishers, 199 W. 8th Ave., Suite 3, Eugene, OR 97401.

Cascade Books
An Imprint of Wipf and Stock Publishers
199 W. 8th Ave., Suite 3
Eugene, OR 97401

www.wipfandstock.com

ISBN 13: 978-1-4982-2087-3

Cataloging-in-Publication data:

Floyd, Richard A.

    Down to earth : Christian hope and climate change / Richard A. Floyd.

    vii + 132 p. ; 23 cm—Includes bibliographical references.

    ISBN 13: 978-1-4982-2087-3

    1. Evolution—Religious aspects—Christianity. 2. Climate change. 3. Eschatology—Christianity. I. Title.

BT712 .F75 2015

Manufactured in the USA.

Scripture quotations are from New Revised Standard Version Bible, copyright © 1989 National Council of the Churches of Christ in the United States of America. Used by permission. All rights reserved.

"The Swan" from *House of Light* by Mary Oliver, published by Beacon Press Boston, copyright © 1990 by Mary Oliver, reprinted by permission of The Charlotte Sheedy Literary Agency Inc.

For Emily, with gratitude, and for Anna and Ella, with hope

Contents

1. Introduction: De-Creation, Re-Creation, New Creation   1
2. Silencing the God of the Whirlwind: Hope and Humility in Jürgen Moltmann   18
3. Subjunctive Faith: Humility and Hope in Sallie McFague   47
4. Taking Our Stand with the Dirt: Humility and the Cosmic Process   74
5. "What Beauty Is For": Hope and the Efficacy of Beauty   98
6. Practicing the New Creation   119

   Bibliography   127

1

Introduction

De-Creation, Re-Creation, New Creation

In late October of 2012 Hurricane ("Superstorm") Sandy cut a swath of destruction along the eastern coast of the United States, inflicting tens of billions of dollars of damage, destroying thousands of homes, leaving millions without power, and causing dozens of fatalities. The National Hurricane Center ranked Hurricane Sandy as the second costliest US hurricane since 1900 (in constant 2010 dollars). The report also noted that, while the number of hurricanes may remain the same or decrease slightly in the near term, the storms that do form are likely to be more intense and destructive due to warming oceans and air.[1] Hurricane Sandy's size, intensity, and trajectory were linked by many analysts to climate change.[2] Its exceedingly unusual interaction with cold "nor'easter" conditions to create a "warm-core nor'easter" (or "frankenstorm") was suggestive of a climate system that was behaving oddly.[3] The storm's surge and deadly flooding were undeniably exacerbated by rising sea levels and coastal erosion. Sandy inflicted catastrophic damage, washing away lives and property—and it was very likely a portent of storms to come in a warming world.

Of course Superstorm Sandy was not the only climate-related story in 2012. Heat waves in Russia, deep drought in China, Brazil, and Australia, and floods in Africa and Pakistan all made the news.[4] Arctic sea ice

---

1. Plumer, "Is Sandy the second-most destructive hurricane ever?"
2. See Nichols, "Has climate change created a monster?"
3. Tobis, "Grim Trajectories."
4. World Meteorological Organization, "Press Release No. 966."

dipped to a minimum in both coverage and volume, reaching the lowest levels in recorded history.[5] As arctic ice reached a record low, greenhouse gas concentrations reached a record high.[6] Unsurprisingly, given this concentration of greenhouse gasses, 2012 proved to be one of the warmest years on record.[7] For many farmers it was a year without a spring, with increased warmth at night eliminating frost and altering the growing season.[8] Drought conditions threatened food production worldwide[9] and contributed to widespread tree mortality.[10] Biodiversity continued to decline: "When it comes down to it, those collapsing glaciers, moving currents and rising sea-levels create so many factors for the equation that is the earth, it is likely we will be too late for the funerals of these unfortunate casualties."[11] Unusual jet stream configurations, still poorly understood, tied together many of these stories: driving Super Stormsandy into New York and New Jersey, bringing killer cold and extreme drought. This may be the "new normal" for air currents in a warming world.[12] Also in 2012, PBS *Frontline* released an exposé on the dirty little secret of huge sums of money flowing from the fossil fuel industry in and through "free market" organizations and conservative think tanks to buy biased studies and clever campaigns of obfuscation in order to "blow doubt into the science."[13] And perhaps the most significant climate story of 2012—significant as a kind of absence—is the 2012 US presidential campaign, which unfolded in the midst of this climate chaos and yet remained resolutely silent about these interconnected issues and the moral imperative to respond to them.

Each of these stories drifted through the news cycle of a single calendar year. 2012 is not exceptional in this regard; similar litanies could be assembled for almost any year in recent memory. Weaving through the disparate stories is the reality of the greenhouse effect, or global warming, or climate change, or global weirding—the nomenclature changes but the

---

5. National Snow & Ice Data Center, "Arctic sea ice extent."
6. World Meteorological Organization, "Press Release No. 965."
7. Met Office, "Met Office 2013 annual global temperature forecast."
8. Laden, "It's the Heat of the Night."
9. Romm, "Brutal Droughts."
10. University of Tennessee, "Dire drought ahead."
11. Armstrong, "Big loss of biodiversity with global warming."
12. Francis and Vavrus, "Evidence linking Arctic amplification to extreme weather in mid-latitudes."
13. Nichols, "'Climate of Doubt'—Money Buys Skepticism."

INTRODUCTION

underlying reality is stubbornly resilient. And stubbornly subtle—so subtle, in fact, that it fails to pierce the consciousness, both because it works on scales outsized for the human brain (at least unaided by science) and because we have a deeply vested interest in not seeing this particular pattern. It is possible—though perhaps it takes a measure of willful ignorance, abetted by an industry devoted to dissembling and denial and a media obsessed with the titillating and the trivial—it is possible to recite this litany of ruin from 2012 or any other year and fail to see the pattern, to miss the forest for the (dying) trees, to interpret the news items as a series of unfortunate events rather than the signs of the times (Matt 16:3).

This climate chaos, caused by idolatrous indifference and concupiscent consumption, brings to mind another word, a word that better captures the deep and systemic unraveling of the intricately interconnected web of earthly life that the human creature is now perpetrating: de-creation. Of course de-creation, like creation, is properly only an act of God. Human beings are certainly well on their way to eliminating the conditions of existence for themselves and for countless other species, but they lack the power to undo creation itself. Even as the earth is deeply impoverished by human indifference and consumption, it continues to spin madly on—as do all the other planets surrounding all the other stars in this incomprehensibly vast creation.

But if creation means not simply all that is but also the ordering of all that is toward the divine end, and if that divine end includes the cultivation of beauty and the impartation of divine love, then the human creature may or may not be able to finally thwart such an end, but it can at the very least make it a far more torturous process. And while the human creature may not be able to unravel the web of existence throughout all time and space, it can certainly desecrate the only home it has. So perhaps the word *de-creation* has some traction after all.

De-creation in this (perhaps more local) sense is a not-uncommon theme in the Old Testament.[14] "The fields are devastated, the ground mourns; for the grain is destroyed, the wine dries up, the oil fails," weeps the prophet Joel (1:10). Divine judgment is at hand, and only fasting and weeping and mourning ("rend your hearts and not your clothing" [2:13])

---

14. There are important debates about how one references the "Old Testament" or the "Hebrew Bible," etc. Without diving deeply into these tumultuous waters, I will say that I use "Old Testament" not to reinforce supercessionist readings of the text (or history) but rather to confess that I (inevitably) read this text with Christian assumptions and biases, though hopefully also critically and with as much integrity as I can manage.

will cause God to relent, such that once again "the pastures of the wilderness are green; the tree bears its fruit, the fig tree and vine give their full yield" (2:22). The prophet Jeremiah asks, "How long will the land mourn, and the grass of every field wither? For the wickedness of those who live in it the animals and the birds are swept away, and because people said, 'He is blind to our ways'" (Jer 12:4). The people imagined they could live autonomous lives, supremely unconcerned with covenantal fidelity, fidelity to God and to neighbor and to creation itself—and because of this, the animals suffer and the grass withers. In Deuteronomy, among the litany of curses the Lord will deliver upon those who are disobedient is the warning that:

> The Lord will afflict you with consumption, fever, inflammation, with fiery heat and drought, and with blight and mildew; they shall pursue you until you perish. The sky over your head shall be bronze, and the earth under you iron. The Lord will change the rain of your land into powder, and only dust shall come down upon you from the sky until you are destroyed (Deut 28:22–24).

The prophet Hosea similarly envisions a close and costly connection between the desolation of the land and the faithfulness of the people:

> Hear the word of the Lord, O people of Israel; for the Lord has an indictment against the inhabitants of the land. There is no faithfulness or loyalty, and no knowledge of God in the land. Swearing, lying, and murder, and stealing and adultery break out; bloodshed follows bloodshed. Therefore the land mourns, and all who live in it languish; together with the wild animals and the birds of the air, even the fish of the sea are perishing (Hos 4:1–3).

Perhaps the greatest testimony to de-creation in the Old Testament is found in Jeremiah. The *tohu va vohu* ("waste and void") of Jeremiah 4:23 occurs only one other time in the Old Testament: the "formless void" of Genesis 1 out of which God creates. Jeremiah's vision is an almost complete devolution of creation to a primordial state of chaos.

> I looked on the earth, and lo, it was waste and void; and to the heavens, and they had no light. I looked on the mountains, and lo, they were quaking, and all the hills moved to and fro. I looked, and lo, there was no one at all, and all the birds of the air had fled. I looked, and lo, the fruitful land was a desert, and all its cities were laid in ruins before the Lord, before his fierce anger. For thus says the Lord: The whole land shall be a desolation; yet I will not make a full end. Because of this the earth shall mourn, and the heavens

above grow black; for I have spoken, I have purposed; I have not relented nor will I turn back (Jer 4:23–28).

Similarly in the New Testament we find Paul's vision of the "groaning of creation" in Romans 8:18–23. At times this text has been interpreted in ways that cannot easily be reconciled with what we know of biological history (e.g., suggestions that the text points to a fundamental change in the structure of the natural world following human sin and the "fall" of Genesis 3). Nevertheless, Paul clearly envisions a breakdown of the created order (or, better, orderings), the earth groaning in travail under the awful weight of human concupiscence.

These texts tie together the health and peace (the "shalom") of creation, the fidelity of the human creature, and the judgment of God in complex and disconcerting ways. At times it seems to be simply a matter of the causality inherent in creation itself: the earth warms, glaciers melt, sea levels rise, storms become more intense, devastation follows. At other times the text seems to posit divine action as the mechanism of judgment. Ellen Davis notes that these texts presuppose a "biblical understanding of the world, in which the physical, moral, and spiritual orders fully interpenetrate one another—in contrast to modern superstition that these are separable categories."[15] Fair enough. But we are rightly troubled by the terribly indiscriminate nature of the judgments rendered here. Why do the vulnerable innocent suffer disproportionately when judgment falls on the mighty? As a prescription for divine agency, it is reprehensible. As a description of what is in fact the case, it is tragically perceptive.

However we sort out the thorny constellation of creation's fecundity, humanity's concupiscence, and divine agency, these texts point to the possibility of de-creation (at least in the local sense): the unraveling of the web of creation due to the human creatures' propensity to burst beyond the bounds of covenantal fidelity, to "live beyond their limits." Scientists have long warned about the possibility of human beings overshooting the carrying capacity of the earth; long before that, the Bible mused about the possibility of human beings overshooting the covenantal responsibilities by which creation was harmoniously maintained, with devastating consequences not only for the human creature but for the land and the sea and all the creatures of the earth.

---

15. Davis, *Scripture, Culture, and Agriculture*, 9–10.

This is certainly not the only vision to be found in the text. Other texts render other possibilities for the human creature in the midst of creation. Psalm 148 implores the human creature to add its voice to the ecstatic and erotic song of praise that vibrates throughout the cosmos: angels, sun and moon, stars, heavens, waters, earth, sea monsters, fire and hail, snow and frost, mountains and hills, fruit trees and cedars, wild animals and cattle, creeping things and flying birds, kings and princes, young men and women, old and young alike—all add their particular tone and rhythm to the song. This vision of all creatures exulting and celebrating is quite common in the text.[16] Brian Swimme and Thomas Berry take this to be the very heart of existence itself.

> If we were to choose a single expression for the universe it might be "celebration," celebration of existence and life and consciousness, also of color and sound but especially in movement, in flight through the air and swimming through the sea, in mating rituals and care of the young.... The universe as a community of diverse components rings with a certain exultation and joy in being.... Everything about us seems to be absorbed into a vast celebratory experience. Whatever be the more practical purposes of existence it appears that celebration is omnipresent, not simply in the individual modes of its expression but in the grandeur of the entire cosmic process.[17]

Of course we hasten to add that this "vast celebratory experience" is also riddled with affliction and suffering. The beauty of creation is gracefully intertwined with the tragic. The song of praise has discordant tones and mournful countermelodies. Granting this, time and again the text calls the human creature to take its place among the teeming multitude of creatures, to add its voice to the song.

Psalm 104 sings of the orderings of creation, with every creature having its time and place in the great cosmic symphony. The psalm praises the fecundity of divine creativity, marveling at the panoply of creatures, the diversity of species, the ways they are interconnected and yet distinct. God provides to every creature breath, water, food, time, place, and joy. God provides prey for the lion (v. 21), suggesting that predation is a wild but necessary part of the good creation. Death is accepted as simply part of the natural ordering of things (v. 29). Water is a pervasive theme in this psalm:

---

16. Fretheim, *God and the World in the Old Testament*, 267–78, lists fifty such texts.
17. Swimme and Berry, *Universe Story*, 263–64.

"you make the springs gush forth in the valleys; they flow between the hills, giving drink to every wild animal" (v. 10). Every creature has its time and place: the sun goes down and "all the animals of the forest come creeping out" (v. 20); the sun comes up and "people go out to their work and to their labor until the evening" (v. 23).

The place of the human creatures in Psalm 104 is noteworthy. They take their place as one among the many other animals, enjoying their time and space. But the very end of the psalm points to the only threat to the exquisite orderings of creation: the "sinners" and the "wicked" (v. 35). In this case human exceptionalism appears to mean that humans have the exceptional capacity to despoil and disrupt creation. As Walter Brueggemann writes, sinners

> are those who refuse to receive life in creation on terms of generous extravagance, no doubt in order to practice a hoarding autonomy in denial that creation is indeed governed and held by its Creator. Creation has within it the sovereign seriousness of God, who will not tolerate the violation of the terms of creation, which are terms of gift, dependence and extravagance.[18]

Thus Psalm 104 stands as a kind of hinge between the prophets of de-creation and the promises of a doxological creation where every creature has its time and space and the divine creativity sustains life and breath and food and water and beauty and joy. Which way the hinge falls depends largely on the final disposition of the human creature in verse 35.

Sadly, the human creature seems determined to play the role of the despoiler, to "practice a hoarding autonomy," to overshoot the covenantal responsibilities that make possible the life-sustaining orderings of Psalm 104. The annual report of the World Meteorological Organization reads like a litany of climate chaos.[19] The report notes that, while 2013 was not the hottest year on record (it was in the top ten), thirteen of fourteen of the world's hottest years since records have been kept have occurred in the twenty-first century. Each decade of the last three decades has been hotter than the one before it, with 2001 to 2010 being the hottest decade on record. Climate scientists are increasingly confident in linking these rising temperatures to an increase in the likelihood of extreme weather. For example:

---

18. Brueggemann, *Theology of the Old Testament*, 156.
19. World Meteorological Organization, "WMO Statement."

[C]omparing climate model simulations with and without human factors shows that the record hot Australian summer of 2012/13 was about five times as likely as a result of human-induced influence on climate and that the record hot calendar year of 2013 would have been virtually impossible without human contributions of heat-trapping gases, illustrating that some extreme events are becoming much more likely due to climate change.[20]

In other words, we are loading the climate dice.

Other findings from the 2013 WMO report:

- Typhoon Haiyan (Yolanda), one of the strongest storms to ever make landfall, devastated parts of the central Philippines
- Surface air temperatures over land in the southern hemisphere were very warm, resulting in widespread heat waves; Australia saw record warmth for the year, Argentina its second warmest year, and New Zealand its third warmest
- Frigid polar air swept across parts of Europe and the southeastern United States
- Severe drought gripped Angola, Botswana, and Namibia
- Heavy monsoon rains led to severe floods on the India-Nepal border
- Abundant rains and flooding impacted northeastern China and the eastern Russian Federation
- Heavy rains and floods affected Sudan and Somalia
- Major drought affected southern China
- Northeastern Brazil experienced its worst drought in the past 50 years
- The widest tornado ever observed hit El Reno, Oklahoma, in the United States
- Extreme precipitation led to severe floods in the Alps and in Austria, the Czech Republic, Germany, Poland, and Switzerland
- Israel, Jordan, and the Syrian Arab Republic were struck by unprecedented snowfall
- An extra-tropical windstorm affected several countries in western and northern Europe

20. Ibid.

- Greenhouse gas concentrations in the atmosphere reached record highs
- The global oceans reached new record high sea levels
- The Antarctic sea ice extent reached a record daily maximum[21]

These indisputable facts on the ground are suggestive of a creation that is drifting from the salubrious orderings of Psalm 104 into turmoil.

Global emissions of greenhouse gasses reached a record high in 2012.[22] Gupta et al.[23] argue that emissions need to be 25 percent to 40 percent *below* 1990 levels by 2020 in order to limit global warming to below 2 degrees Celsius relative to preindustrial temperature levels. The 2012 level was 58 percent *above* 1990 levels. Rising greenhouse gases contribute to increasing temperatures, causing the waters that flow so freely in Psalm 104 to dry up. The three biggest grain producers—China, India, and the United States—and fifteen other countries (totaling half of the world's population) are overdrawing their aquifers, some to the point that the aquifers are being depleted and wells are drying up.[24] California is facing what may be its worst drought in four decades; more than 90 percent of the state is suffering from severe or extreme drought (some estimates now say it is greater than 99 percent of the state).[25] According to the United Nations roughly 1.2 billion people around the world (one-fifth of the world's population) are affected by water scarcity; that number is expected to reach 1.8 billion by 2025.[26]

In Psalm 104 God gives creatures "their food in due season." But a report by the IPCC warns that increasing temperatures, while having some beneficial effects on crop growth in some locales, will make it harder for crops to thrive globally, reducing production by as much as 2 percent each decade for the rest of this century. During this same period, demand is expected to rise as much as 14 percent each decade, as the world population continues to grow.[27] As with the emission of greenhouse gases, the numbers are moving in the wrong direction.

21. Ibid.
22. Auth, "Record High for Global Greenhouse Gas Emissions."
23. Gupta et al., "Chapter 13."
24. Brown, "Peak Water."
25. West, "Check Out This Shocking Map of California's Drought."
26. Shabad, "Water scarcity escalating due to climate change, report says."
27. Gillis, "Climate Change Seen Posing Risk to Food Supplies." The official report

The Climate Vulnerability Report estimates that climate change causes 400,000 deaths each year, related to hunger and communicable diseases (affecting above all children in developing countries); by 2030 this figure is expected to reach more than 600,000. The report also estimates that climate change has already cost the world close to 1 percent of global GDP; by 2030 these costs could exceed 3 percent global GDP.[28]

A report in the journal *Nature* draws out the role of climate change in triggering and exacerbating conflict: "What [the research] does show and show beyond any doubt is that even in this modern world, climate variations have an impact on the propensity of people to fight."[29] This analysis of conflict focuses on the prospects of people responding with violence to the loss of land, food, water, and other resources due to climate change, that is, violence "from below." But it could be argued that climate change itself is a form of violence, violence against the earth, against fragile ecosystems, against species, against the poor who in turn react with violence to the loss of their means of survival. This violence "from above" is not perpetrated by the poor but rather by the well-heeled, the politically connected, the complacent, and the comfortable. Corporations have sunk costs into this violent order. As Rebecca Solnit writes:

> In every arena, we need to look at industrial-scale and systemic violence, not just the hands-on violence of the less powerful. When it comes to climate change, this is particularly true. Exxon has decided to bet that we can't make the corporation keep its reserves in the ground, and the company is reassuring its investors that it will continue to profit off the rapid, violent and intentional destruction of the Earth.[30]

Solnit references the remarkably candid report issued by Exxon Mobil on March 31, 2014—the same day the latest (and direst) IPCC report was released. In the report Exxon acknowledges both the reality of climate change and the political pressures it brings to bear, and then discounts them, saying it is "highly unlikely" that government regulations will hinder the full exploitation of their carbon reserves.[31] Exxon Mobil and other energy corporations already have many times more carbon in their reserves

---

has since been released.

28. Climate Vulnerability Report.
29. AFP, "Study proves climate a trigger for conflict."
30. Solnit, "Call climate change what it is: violence."
31. McKibben, "Exxon Mobil's response to climate change is consummate arrogance."

than we can safely burn, and here Exxon assures their stockholders that they will burn through those reserves despite political pressure and despite what it will do the planet.

Earlier research published by the *Proceedings of the National Academy of Sciences* suggests that, in a worst-case scenario of global warming—worst case in 2010; its likelihood has increased since then—much of the world may simply become too hot for humans to live. "We show that even modest global warming could therefore expose large fractions of the population to unprecedented heat stress, and that with severe warming this would become intolerable."[32]

The recent report from the American Association for the Advancement of Science summarizes the situation: "The evidence is overwhelming: Levels of greenhouse gases in the atmosphere are rising. Temperatures are going up. Springs are arriving earlier. Ice sheets are melting. Sea level is rising. The patterns of rainfall and drought are changing. Heat waves are getting worse, as is extreme precipitation. The oceans are acidifying."[33] As one of the authors of the recently released IPCC report on the impacts of climate change said: "The horrible is something quite likely, and we won't be able to do anything about it."[34]

How does one cultivate hope in the face of such de-creation? The blessings and woes of Deuteronomy presupposed an agent capable of choosing the way of life or the way of death. Similarly, many of the prophets of de-creation proclaim that there is still time, that destruction may be forestalled if the people will but return to covenantal fidelity. But other texts suggest that things are too far gone, that the human creature has turned every inclination of its heart to de-creation, first de-creating itself and then other creatures, and that it is only by divine agency—in judgment and redemption—that hope is possible. The human animal run amuck is a threat to creation. Psalm 104 does not exhort the human animal to straighten up and find its place and time within the dance of creation. No, it calls down divine judgment: "let sinners be consumed from the earth, and let the wicked by no more" (Ps 104:35).

Perhaps in a more promising mode we find the prophet Isaiah. If Jeremiah 4:23–28 is the archetypal text of de-creation, perhaps Isaiah 35 is the

32. Rice, "Report."
33. AAAS Climate Science Panel, "What We Know."
34. Borenstein, "UN report dials up humanity's global warming risks; scientist says 'We're all sitting ducks.'"

archetypal text of re-creation. "The wilderness and the dry land shall be glad, the desert shall rejoice and blossom; like the crocus it shall blossom abundantly, and rejoice with joy and singing . . . . For waters shall break forth in the wilderness, and streams in the desert" (Isa 35:1–2a, 6b). Here the people have suffered through the devastation of de-creation and at long last the wetness and fecundity of Psalm 104 is being restored; the ecstatic singing of Psalm 148 is being heard again. It is understood to be the work of God, to be sure, but the prophet casts the vision, and the people must rise up and move toward it.

Isaiah 65:17–25 is another text of re-creation. It is not merely a restatement of the fundamentally gracious orderings of creation, as in Psalm 104, nor is it a call for all creatures to join in doxological ecstasy, as in Psalm 148. It is, rather, the promise of something new, a newness brought about by divine creativity.

> For I am about to create new heavens and a new earth; the former things shall not be remembered or come to mind. But be glad and rejoice forever in what I am creating; for I am about to create Jerusalem as a joy, and its people as a delight. I will rejoice in Jerusalem, and delight in my people; no more shall the sound of weeping be heard in it, or the cry of distress (Isa 65:17–19).

Such language may invite a Marxist analysis. Do not such eschatological flights of fancy eviscerate the will to act with courage and compassion in the here and now? Perhaps. But this is not a vision of a far-flung future. The tense of the verb *bara* (create) suggests that this re-creation is not simply a future project (as the NRSV translation suggests) but a present and unfolding process: "I am creating . . . ". And what is being created is remarkably "down to earth": no more infant mortality or premature death (v. 20); people build houses and get to live in them and plant crops and get to eat them (vv. 21–22); children are not born into poverty or calamity (v. 23a); there is neither "destructive threat nor competitive anxiety," but rather the promise that "God will bless and make the force of life everywhere palpably available."[35] It is only as the text reaches its climax that it begins to drift in poetic ecstasy beyond the bounds of the earth as we know it (or can readily imagine it), with pacifist wolves and straw-eating lions (v. 25).

In the New Testament, Revelation 21 intentionally echoes Isaiah 65. It too promises a new heaven and a new earth—only here re-creation has become *new* creation. The new is a renovation of the old in Isaiah 65; in

---

35. Brueggemann, *Threat of Life*, 65–66.

Revelation 21 the new is more nearly a negation of the old: "for the first heaven and the first earth had passed away" (v. 1a). One may read the re-creation of Isaiah 65 as coming "from below" ("the force of life everywhere palpably available," as Brueggemann put it above), whereas the new creation of Revelation 21 comes "from above": "the holy city, the new Jerusalem, come down out of heaven from God, prepared as a bride adorned for her husband" (v. 2).

Perhaps most divergent in these two visions is the place of death in the renewed/new creation. Isaiah 65 imagines the eradication of infant mortality and premature death, death due to violent usurpation, the death that comes from ruptured relations with the community and with the divine. These modes of "bad" death have been extirpated from creation, but not death itself, not death as the natural end of finite creatures. The days of the people will be "like the days of a tree," but even trees die. Echoing Psalm 104, death remains a natural part of God's good creation in Isaiah 65.

In Revelation 21, however, death itself—not premature death or violent death or unjust death, but *all* death—has been eliminated: "Death will be no more" (4b). Of course Revelation 21 also echoes Isaiah 25, and Isaiah 25:8 ventured that "[God] will swallow up death forever." But Revelation 21 takes this promise one step further. It is not enough to declare that "death will be no more," because death (at least in this vision) is inextricably woven together with a chaotically disordered creation. In order to destroy death, God must destroy the chaos that clings to finitude itself. And so verse 1b: "the sea was no more." The sea is commonly a symbol of turmoil and chaos in biblical texts, going all the way back to the "face of the waters" over which the spirit of God hovered in Genesis 1. If creation emerges out of this watery chaos, then the threat of being subsumed lingers. Jesus may temporarily rebuke the watery chaos (cf. Matt 8:23–27), but only in the vision of Revelation 21 is it finally eliminated.[36]

My project is located at the nexus of these themes: the de-creation of which we are both perpetrators and victims; the complex and ambiguous interconnections between creation's fecundity, humanity's concupiscence, and divine creativity; and the hopeful but at times discordant visions of re-creation and new creation. In the face of global weirding and ecological diminishment, in the face of de-creation, how can we hope—and hope in

36. These themes are traced out with depth and nuance in Keller, *Face of the Deep*.

such a way that creation itself, good and beautiful, marked by tragedy and chaos—is taken up rather than left behind? This is a particularly pointed question for the Christian tradition. Research published in the *Political Science Quarterly* confirms what many thinkers at the nexus of religion and ecology have long supposed, that particular Christian theological claims—in this case belief in the "second coming"—stifle climate change action.[37] Can a Christian vision—a vision which has at times been drunk on eschatological dreams (or nightmares) that consign this world and most of its creatures to the flames—can a Christian vision foster an earthly hope?

Many have argued that this question must be answered in the negative. Lynn White's 1967 essay, "The Historical Roots of Our Ecologic Crisis," indicted the Christian tradition for fostering an exploitative attitude toward nature.[38] White contended that the dominion tradition of Genesis 1 in conjunction with the medieval monastic emphasis on holy work laid the "psychic foundations" for industry run amuck. In the years following, others have deepened White's critique, claiming that the Christian doctrine of creation was deeply anthropocentric, rendering humanity the measure of all things; or that a transcendent *summum bonum* drained intrinsic value from nature; or else that Christian apocalypticism rendered the earth expendable in the divine drama of human redemption. Christian eco-theologians such as Jürgen Moltmann and Sallie McFague have responded creatively and powerfully to these charges. However, the question of an earthly hope, a "down-to-earth" eschatology, remains unsettled.

The ecological crisis itself raises eschatological questions, in two senses. First, insofar as eschatology illuminates the ultimate end of all things in terms of *telos*, then the ecological crisis is an eschatological crisis—that is, a crisis of meaning, purpose, and value. Our utilitarian valuing of creation, even (or especially) our theological construals of creation as the object of human dominion, are among the roots of our present ecological predicament. A humble eschatology (humble in the etymological sense of "close to the earth"; *humus* = land, soil), an eschatology rooted in the intrinsic value of creation and the integrity of its life-before-God, is a necessary constructive response.

The ecological crisis raises eschatological questions in a second sense. Insofar as eschatology illuminates the ultimate end of all things in terms of *finis*, then our ecological crisis raises the eschatological specter of

---

37. Dolan, "Belief in biblical end-times stifling climate change action in U.S."
38. White, "The Historical Roots of Our Ecologic Crisis."

eco-apocalypse and "the end of the world." As we have seen, scientists are issuing increasingly dire warnings about the climate we are creating for our children, their children, and the other-than-human creatures who share it. Some voices of Christian apocalyptic join in the refrain in their own key, preaching that the disintegration of creation is a necessary prelude to God's new creation. However, a hopeful eschatology, an eschatology that affirms the ever-present possibility of renewal because of the divine creativity in the midst of creation, is a necessary aspect of any Christian response to the ecological crisis.

The eschatological questions raised by the ecological crisis—questions of *telos* and *finis*—point to two lacunae in Christian eschatology, namely, the ambiguous affirmation of the present intrinsic value of creation (often figured as an initial created goodness that was subsequently lost, or a soon-to-be goodness that stands in contradiction to present reality), and the precarious affirmation of hope and divine creativity in the midst of a collapsing ecosystem. Our eschatological response to the ecological crisis must be both humble—grounded in creation—and hopeful—grounded in the divine creativity.

In order to map the landscape of these two trajectories, I engage the work of Jürgen Moltmann (chapter 2) and Sallie McFague (chapter 3). These two figures have worked extensively on the doctrine of creation in the context of the ecological crisis and have developed diverse—and, from my perspective, ultimately inadequate—eschatologies in response.

Moltmann's[39] eschatological vision has a vast sweep, and he endeavors to inscribe creation within that vision at every turn. However, ultimately his vision cannot quite escape a latent asymmetry in the Christian tradition, where creation incorporates all things, but redemption and eschatological fulfillment are focused primarily on the human creature. It cannot be insignificant that Moltmann's final eschatological vision is a city.[40] Note that this occurs at the conclusion of his discussion of *cosmic* eschatology. We might expect the city to be the apotheosis of human historical existence, but of cosmic existence? Is the whole purpose of the cosmos the provision of a habitable environment for the human creature? Moltmann makes space for nature in the new creation, but it is human space (city-space). Creation

---

39. Eschatological themes weave throughout Moltmann's work. My analysis will focus on *The Coming of God*, where eschatology itself becomes the subject of theological analysis, and *God in Creation*, where Moltmann's eschatological orientation most clearly intersects with his (and my) ecological concerns.

40. Moltmann, *Coming of God*, 308–19.

exists in the eschaton only as a garden, a symbol of the human cultivation of nature.[41] The wilderness, where creation dwells in and for itself and has its own life before God, is no more. Creation endures now only as a human construct. Thus we see that, despite Moltmann's fervent efforts to hold creation within the narrative of redemption, what we actually find there is a de-natured nature, a humanized nature. In the terms I have been developing, Moltmann's eschatology is deeply hopeful, but it is not humble.

While eschatology is the dominant key in much of Moltmann's work, for McFague[42] it is a minor key (or perhaps a counter-melody) that weaves in and out of her other reflections. At times she can echo Moltmann in her effusive hopefulness, speaking of God's Spirit transforming the entire body (the universe) toward reconciliation and peace. But ultimately her affirmations of hope are tied to conditional human responses. On the one hand this sustains the humble dimensions of McFague's eschatology: she does not envision a divine unmaking and remaking of the world. Whatever hopeful future the world has is tied to the divine initiative, to be sure, but it is channeled through and limited by human creatures. There will be no new Jerusalem descending from the heavens, and, by extension, there will be no vegetarian lions. What will be is limited to what human creatures, called and inspired by God, can accomplish. On the other hand this conditional vision is what finally prevents McFague's eschatology from being truly hopeful. Her affirmation of what she calls postmodern science over against any kind of divine *ex nihilo* creative power has already reduced her horizons: the sun will burn out, all life on earth will end. Combined with her insistence that new creation, limited though it may be, comes about only in and through human creatures, the hopefulness of her vision is attenuated.

Thus Moltmann and McFague offer two possibilities for an ecological eschatology: one that privileges the Christian narrative (and especially the Easter narrative) and so is deeply hopeful and cosmic in its intent but cannot quite shake the anthropocentrism and asymmetry that has long stalked Christian eschatological reflection; the other privileging the patterns and processes discernible in human existence in nature as the ground for discerning God's power, thus staying close to the ground (humble) but ultimately despairing of any transcendent powers that might create new

---

41. Ibid., 313–15.

42. My analysis of McFague will focus primarily on her central metaphorical venture as found in *The Body of God*, though it will necessarily draw on many other strands of her work given the ad hoc nature of her eschatology.

INTRODUCTION

possibilities not already immanent within cosmic processes. In my judgment, neither eschatological vision is sufficient. Thus I argue that the challenge remains for ecotheology: to come "down to earth"; that is, to articulate an ecological eschatology that is both humble and hopeful, grounded in creation and in the divine creativity.

In chapters 4 and 5 I take some faltering steps in response to this challenge. In chapter 4 I consider more fully the category of humility, arguing that to be humble is to remain ever mindful of the ways our origin and destiny are inextricably interwoven with the origin and destiny of dirt. Of course dirt is never simply dirt: it opens out to the entire cosmic process. If humility means staying grounded, standing in solidarity with the dirt, then it also means standing in solidarity with the entire cosmic process in which it and we are embedded. I argue that the cosmic process in which we are embedded is mysterious and contingent; good and graced; evolving, emerging, and dynamic. It is not centered on the human creature, though the human creature has a place and a time within it, and it is tragically structured, creative advance through perpetual perishing, with the very goods of creaturely existence entailing suffering. Humility in the sense I am developing means consent to *this* creation, not some other.

In chapter 5 the discussion turns to hope. What are the grounds for hope in the midst of ecological diminishment? How can we hope in such a way that we maintain our humility, our solidarity with the dirt? How can we hope in such a way that nature is taken up into our hopes rather than being de-natured or left behind? I weave my discussion of hope around the theological foci of God, self, and world. God is "the hope of all the ends of the earth and of the farthest sea" (Ps 65:5b). As we have seen, that hope manifests itself in both judgment and redemption. But it takes root only in a redeemed self, that is, a self that has relinquished its grasp on the idols of proximate goods and has been set free from endlessly destructive strategies for self-securing, a self that has been founded in God. In the end I argue that our hope is finally to be found in beauty, the fragile beauty of each creature that evokes wonder and compassion, the beauty of a redeemed self that has been set free to go out in love for the other, and the beauty of God that lures forth ever-new, fecund possibilities and gathers up all the beautiful and broken creatures into the deepest possible harmony.

2

Silencing the God of the Whirlwind
Hope and Humility in Jürgen Moltmann

The question of hope—its possibility, its urgency, its disruptive and transformative power—has animated the writings of Jürgen Moltmann from the very beginning. From his first major work, proclaiming that "those who hope in Christ can no longer put up with reality as it is, but begin to suffer under it, to contradict it,"[1] to his most recent work, calling for hopeful resistance in the midst of "endangered life, the threatened earth, and the lack of justice and righteousness,"[2] a hopeful orientation toward God's future has been a touchstone for Moltmann's thought.

The question of hope for Moltmann is intertwined with, indeed almost synonymous with, the question of a Christian eschatology. He joins those who lament the loss of eschatology in nineteenth- and early twentieth-century Christian theology. Ernst Troeltsch quipped that in his day "the eschatological office is closed most of the time."[3] Karl Barth bemoaned a Protestant theology lulled "comfortably to sleep by adding to the conclusion of Christian Dogmatics a short and perfectly harmless chapter entitled—Eschatology."[4] Barth himself, along with Rudolf Bultmann and others, instigated a radical reorientation of eschatology, moving it from the harmless conclusion of dogmatics to a central category, one that marks the presence of eternity in every moment and the need for decision when

---

1. Moltmann, *Theology of Hope*, 21.
2. Moltmann, *Ethics of Hope*, xii.
3. Cited by Schwöbel, "Last Things First?," 217.
4. Barth, *Epistle to the Romans*, 500.

confronted with kerygma. But this radical reorientation proved unsatisfactory to Moltmann. It neglected actual historical conditions and cultivated a discarnate hope, one that threatened to leave behind historical exigencies and creative material possibilities. For Moltmann, hope in less than the restoration of *all things* is less than Christian hope.

But what does restoration entail? *From what* must creation be restored? Is creation fallen, marred and warped by sin? Is it incomplete, a promise of something yet to come? Is it beautiful and broken, calling forth compassion and humble consent, despite its tragic structures, despite its "negativities," despite its powers and orderings that are at times inimical to the human creature?

This tension drives my engagement with Moltmann (and my question more broadly). How does one articulate an incarnate hope, a hope that encompasses all things, without doing violence to their fragile particularities? How does one envision a restoration of all things that does not obliterate apparent negativities, negativities which may in fact be the *sine qua non* of a good and evolving creation?

Put another way: Moltmann walks the fault line between a hopeful orientation toward the future and a humble cherishing of the good, green earth. He is sensitive to the ways eschatological visions can project an ambivalent if not dismissive orientation toward material creation, and he labors to make sure that the hopeful sweep of his vision takes up rather than obliterates all the many beautiful and broken creatures of the earth. The central question, however, is whether or not this labor is finally successful.

Hope in an open future grounded in divine creativity, and solidarity with a beautiful and fragile creation: these are the threads I will be weaving together in what follows. I am not engaging Moltmann's eschatology as a discrete theological doctrine, for many of the considerations that traditionally fall under the Christian doctrine of eschatology (the last judgment, heaven and hell, the [second] parousia, etc.) are at most tangential to my primary concerns. However, an engagement with eschatological trajectories in Moltmann is inevitable and fruitful—inevitable because eschatology is the key for all Christian theology for Moltmann ("the medium of Christian faith as such, the key in which everything in it is set, the glow that suffuses everything here in the dawn of an unexpected new day"[5]), and fruitful because eschatology raises the questions of hope and the suffering of creation with particular force and clarity.

---

5. Moltmann, "My Theological Career," 170.

An Untamed Garden: Moltmann's Methodology

Engagement with Moltmann's work is a daunting task, as he has been frightfully prolific over an extended period of time. His commitment to contextualization gives his theology a peripatetic quality ("the road emerged only as I walked it"[6]), ever "fragmentary and unfinished" as it responds to the exigencies of creation and history and the fresh winds of the Spirit.[7] Complicating matters is his (for some, maddening) reticence to address methodological questions in a systematic way. He acknowledges the primary role of venturing and imagination in his theology: "the metaphors for experiences of God in history have to be flexible, so that they invite us to voyage into the future and encourage us to seek the kingdom of God."[8] This emphasis on imagination, metaphor, and experience and the experimental, poetic, even playful dimension they bring to theological reflection will be helpful points of contact for our engagement with Sallie McFague's work in the next chapter. For now, however, they leave us struggling to find our methodological footing.

Joy Ann McDougall has helpfully identified three leitmotifs in Moltmann's theology. She characterizes his theology, first, as having "a biblical foundation and a narrative structure."[9] The particularities of the biblical text give a fragmentary and ragged shape to theology; thus it cannot be subsumed under any single scheme—methodological, ontological, or otherwise. The second and third leitmotifs flow directly from the first. Moltmann's theology is, second, "a soteriological doctrine in an eschatological key"[10]—focused with particular force on the narrative of the cross as an event of divine solidarity and pathos and the resurrection as the inbreaking of the *novum*-making power of God. Third, McDougall describes Moltmann's theology as characterized by "the praxis of trinitarian faith."[11]

McDougall sees this third leitmotif playing out in two crucial trajectories. First is the political, where the cross is seen as the unmasking of the idolatrous "monotheistic" god of much modern theology, a god that is a perfect totem for bourgeois political religion. Moltmann instead offers

---

6. Moltmann, *Experiences in Theology*, xv.
7. Ibid., xvi.
8. Moltmann, *Spirit of Life*, 301.
9. McDougall, *Pilgrimage of Love*, 11.
10. Ibid., 13.
11. Ibid., 16.

trinitarian theology as a model for social relations of mutuality and differentiation.[12] Second is the doxological, where play and piety serve as a renewing and critical dialectical partner with political activism.[13] "Without the free play of imagination and songs of praise, the new obedience deteriorates into legalism . . . . But without concrete obedience, which means without physical, social, and political changes, the lovely songs and celebrations of freedom become empty phrases."[14]

Weaving these three leitmotifs together, Moltmann's theology can be seen as a deeply rooted but somewhat untamed garden. The biblical narrative winds through his work, fused with extra-narrative extrapolations (his reflections on intra-trinitarian relations, for example), and yet this rootedness in the text does not produce a monolithic orthodoxy but rather an untamed profusion of imaginative wagers, creative excurses, and passionate proposals, all held together by the story of the triune God making all things new. Such an untamed theological garden can be difficult to explore. So we return to the central question, or rather, the central constellation of questions: a hopeful orientation toward the future and a humble solidarity with creation. I will use these as touch points in my exploration of Moltmann.

In what follows I will look first at Moltmann's discussion of natural theology. This brings to the surface Moltmann's creative grounding in the Reformed tradition, his concern that a Cartesian dualism stalks both Christian theology and secular culture (with deleterious consequences for human and other-than-human creatures), and his commitment to relocate the doctrine of creation within a larger eschatological narrative. Next I will turn to Moltmann's discussion of eschatology proper, the distortions of it that have plagued the Christian tradition, and the nested spheres of personal, historical, and cosmic eschatology that encapsulate his hope for the restoration of all things. Finally I will sketch out four additional eschatological perspectives, each configuring the tension between hope and humility in a different way, in order to cast Moltmann's particular vision into sharper relief.

Throughout I will be exploring the possibilities and the limitations of Moltmann's vision. There is no denying the passionate hopefulness of his vision, rooted in the biblical testimony to the *novum*-making power

---

12. A proposal critiqued by Kathryn Tanner in *Christ the Key*, 207–47.
13. McDougall, *Pilgrimage of Love*, 16–22.
14. Moltmann, *Theology and Joy*, 62.

of God. But does such a vision engender or endanger solidarity with and humble consent to a beautiful, fragile, and tragic creation?

"A Symbol of Its Future": Moltmann's Natural Theology

The question of the nature, the function, and even the possibility of natural theology has been particularly contentious in Reformed theological circles. While giving the Gifford lectures, Karl Barth consistently put the words "natural theology" in quotation marks, pointedly suggesting that the words exist but the reality does not, something like a "unicorn."[15] Is knowledge of God possible antecedent to and/or independent of the special revelation of God? This question raises many broader issues: the particularity of the Christian message vis-à-vis other ways of knowing; the communicability of the Christian message (Tillich suggested Barth's denial of natural theology was akin to treating the Christian message as a rock to be hurled at people); even the heart of the Christian message (natural theology being linked with a kind of "works righteousness" that threatens the "gospel of grace").

Moltmann could profitably be read as a Reformed attempt to move beyond Emil Brunner and Karl Barth in their famous contestation over this question, and to do so in the context of the ecological crisis. He suggests that the ecological crisis and the latent nihilism toward nature that infects modern culture raise the question of natural theology in a new way.[16] If the divine disclosure is strictly limited to human texts, human history, and the incarnation of the divine as a human being, then how can nature enter the theological circle except through anthropocentric renderings?

Barth's "Nein!" to natural theology was in truth a condemnation of a culture turned demonic in its will to power. This was a faithful response to his context, but it becomes problematic as a methodological principle. Barth's debate with Brunner pushed nature off of the theological agenda. Nature was turned over to the scientists; theologians turned their attention to salvation history. True, nature continued to be thematized as the "external basis" of the covenant, and Barth expressed admirable humility in his unwillingness to say too much about other-than-human creatures (the "beasts") and their possible communion with God.[17]

---

15. Barr, *Biblical Faith and Natural Theology*, 7.
16. Moltmann, *God in Creation*, xiii.
17. See Karl Barth's discussion in *Church Dogmatics*, III/2.

However, given the ecological crisis and the nihilism toward nature that so infects the modern world, a theological "passing over" of nature, even a theological humility that simply asserts that we do not know, is inadequate. There are ever-new manifestations of the will to power in our industrialized global economy that seek in unbridled concupiscence to consume the earth. This raises the question of natural theology with considerable urgency.

Moltmann is deeply troubled by a scientific method which subjects all natural systems to human will, born of a Cartesian dualism. Descartes's project was to entertain universal doubt unless and until he identified an original principle that could not itself be doubted, and then to rebuild the edifice of knowledge from that foundation through a chain of deductive reasoning. His project was, in a sense, "successful": he found a kind of certainty in the *cogito*; he identified an argument for the existence of God (how else could the idea of the infinite enter the mind?); he affirmed the "Christian" claim for the immortality of the soul; and he carved out a place for science free from dogmatic meddling. But the price was high: "Modern thought starts with the disembodied, solitary thinker, lacking body, external world, and relationships—or at least not certain of their reality."[18] This stripped, solipsistic self is the starting point for all knowing. True, in league with the God who will defeat the demons of doubt and secure the veracity of clear and distinct ideas, the self and God can reconstitute the world. But the Cartesian self is forever alienated from the world.

Blaise Pascal, a contemporary of Descartes, felt acutely this sense of estrangement from a vast and seemingly alien world:

> When I consider the brief span of my life absorbed into the eternity which comes before and after . . . the small space I occupy which I see swallowed up in the infinite immensity of space, spaces of which I know nothing and which know nothing of me, I take fright and am amazed to see myself here rather than there: there is no reason for me to be here rather than there, now rather than then.[19]

Significantly, this sense of being thrown into an alien world, of radical contingency, leads to a hostile antinomy with nature:

---

18. Levin, *Theories of the Self*, 7.
19. Pascal, *Pensées*, 48.

> Man is only a reed, the weakest in nature, but he is a thinking reed. There is no need for the whole universe to take up arms to crush him: a vapor, a drop of water is enough to kill him. But even if the universe were to crush him, man would still be nobler than his slayer because he knows that he is dying and the advantage that the universe has over him. The universe knows none of this.[20]

The Cartesian self is thrown into a vast, alien, hostile world that is a "slayer" out to "crush him."

Of course this may say as much about Pascal's splenetic temperament as about Descartes's project. Descartes saw this alienation of the self from the world as the distancing necessary for mastery. Far from generating existential angst, Descartes thought his method would "render [us] lords and possessors of nature," as he says in part 6 of his *Discourse on Method*. The intense subjectification of human beings corresponded to an equally intense objectification of nature (and the body), requisite for scientific method. Descartes never could figure out how to connect the *res cogitans* of the mind with the *res extensa* of material reality (pineal glandular theories notwithstanding). So we have this slightly eerie picture of the self, the mind, the omnicompetent subject, pulling the strings of a mechanical body and a mechanical world—without any strings.

Moltmann finds this vision more than eerie. As we have seen, it has had disastrous implications for our understanding of nature: nature as an objectified "thing" to which human beings relate as "*maîtres et possesseurs*." The scientific objectification of nature that it engenders "leads to technological exploitation of nature by human beings."[21] It has also distorted our understanding of the human creature. "The non-spiritual view of nature which Descartes especially brought into vogue was bound to result in the non-natural view of the mind and spirit, and the godless view of both."[22] Natural theology is for Moltmann a crucial check on these destructive distortions. "Nature" is exploitable, while "creation" is situated within a larger narrative that sets moral limits and divine imperatives.[23]

Moltmann affirms many of the trajectories that have long shaped the debate around natural theology. God is only imperfectly knowable by the light of nature, but what is known is true knowledge, and all true

---

20. Ibid., 95.
21. Moltmann, *God in Creation*, 27.
22. Ibid., quoting Franz Baader.
23. Ibid., 21.

knowledge leads to communion.[24] Natural knowledge of God is imperfect, so the resulting communion is imperfect, but it is nevertheless communion. However, while natural knowledge of God may convey God's power and wisdom, salvation is only possible through revealed knowledge, that is, the revelation of God in Jesus Christ.[25] But Moltmann develops these themes in his own creative and capacious ways.

Natural theology presently has three functions for Moltmann.[26] First, it serves an *educative function*, pointing beyond itself to the true revelation of God in Jesus Christ. In Tillichian fashion, Moltmann suggests contemplation of nature raises questions that only revelation can answer. Second, natural theology serves a *hermeneutical function*. It is not a proof of faith, but it does establish a field of meaning within which faith becomes comprehensible. Third (and unsurprisingly), natural theology serves an *eschatological function*. That is, as we contemplate ("fallen") nature, we see intimations of the eschatological new creation to come. "The present world is a real symbol of its future."[27] Contemplation of creation awakens us to nature's yearning for redemption, and our own.

Thus Moltmann wants to embed natural theology within eschatology. Natural theology as we presently practice it is contemplation of a "fallen" world yearning for redemption, a world that is no longer God's original creation and not yet God's coming new creation (though, as we will see below, Moltmann is ambivalent regarding nature's "fallenness"). Calvin too, in his commentary on Genesis, develops this notion of all creation yearning for redemption and living by hope (with echoes of Paul in Romans 8). This is one way of reformulating natural theology in our context, namely, embedding it within eschatological salvation history. This brings nature into the divine-human drama of redemption as more than an "external basis" of the covenant. All creatures, not simply human ones, are on the way to eschatological redemption.

As Moltmann says, nature is more than "merely a parable" (as Barth had suggested); it is a promise, "caught up and absorbed in its own fulfillment."[28] It points beyond itself to its fulfillment in glory. But note well the second clause of Moltmann's sentence: "when what has been promised

---

24. See Moltmann's "relational ontology" in *God in Creation*, 3.
25. Moltmann, *God in Creation*, 57.
26. Ibid., 58–60.
27. Ibid., 56
28. Ibid., 63.

is realized, the promise is discarded."[29] Here we see inklings of Moltmann's ambivalence toward the enduring value of nature: nature, marked as it is by transience and death, is but a broken symbol of God's coming creation.

This approach raises questions. A strong emphasis on eschatological fulfillment seems concomitant with an emphasis on the present fallenness of nature. But it is not clear in what sense we should speak of nature as "fallen." Moltmann makes use of "fall" language in denying that the present condition of creation can be considered "good" in the fullest sense.[30] And yet he also expresses ambivalence:

> Nature has fallen victim to transience and death. It has not fallen through its own sin, like human beings. To talk about a "fallen nature" is therefore highly dubious. And yet a sadness lies over nature which is the expression of its tragic fate and its messianic yearning.[31]

Thus nature is "fallen" because it has not yet attained eschatological fulfillment and because it suffers under the weight of human concupiscence. However, this language of fallenness all too easily elides into a censuring of nature as it is; that is, nature as we have it is either the tattered remnants of a once-pristine creation or the inchoate intimations of a coming new creation. But what of the goodness of creation, not as it was or will be, but as it is?

Moltmann names a "tragic dimension" in nature, but he sees it as a passing shadow that will ultimately be eradicated with the coming of the messianic new day. This question of the place of the tragic within the larger comedic structure of the Christian narrative is crucial and will be explored in a later chapter. But for now, if the concept of a "fallen" creation becomes a means to censure everything in nature that does not conform to human fantasies about how things "should be"—that is, if nature must be "denatured" in order to have a place in eschatological fulfillment—then this approach to natural theology may not be much of an advance—and indeed could be a good bit worse—than a theological "passing over" of nature.

---

29. Ibid.
30. Ibid., 39–40.
31. Ibid., 68.

"Universal Easter Laughter": Moltmann's Eschatology

Jürgen Moltmann endeavors to reinscribe nature (or better, "creation") into the Christian narrative of redemption. He does this primarily by situating personal and historical eschatology within the larger context of cosmic eschatology. But in order to do this, he must successfully navigate many destructive distortions of eschatology. He is acutely aware of the propensity for eschatological visions to become apocalyptic "final solutions" that destroy the meaning of history and the fragile beauty of nature.[32] Given this propensity it is understandable why many would choose to do away with eschatological dreams altogether. But Moltmann finds this equally problematic: "Without God's creative potentialities for the world, worldly potentialities remain determined by presently existing reality and are totally congruent with that."[33] Given the state of "presently existing reality"—human alienation from and destruction of nature and a terminally dysfunctional political system that is unimpeded by concern for the common good—this is counsel for despair. "Our apocalypses are godless, knowing no judgment and no grace, but only the self-inflicted annihilation of humanity."[34] If there is to be hope, the future must be understood not as *futurum* (merely the ongoing realization of natural possibilities) but as *adventus* (the coming of God into history).[35] A Christian eschatology—an eschatology that can take up creation without destroying it—is ground for such hope. It is not about the *end* of things. It is, rather, about the new creation of things.

Moltmann sees two significant distortions of eschatology: transposing eschatology into time and transposing eschatology into eternity. By transposing eschatology into time, he means millenarian and apocalyptic visions that locate eschatology in time rather than understanding eschatology as the transformation of time itself.[36] There will always be an element of millenarianism and apocalypticism in eschatology, the millenarian vision fostering hope by pointing to the new creation, and the apocalyptic vision standing in judgment over all present configurations of power. But millenarianism must not take the form of historical millenarianism, that is, it

---

32. Moltmann, *Coming of God*, x.
33. Moltmann, *God in Creation*, 181.
34. Moltmann, *Coming of God*, 217.
35. Moltmann, "Antwort auf die Kritik der Theologie der Hoffnung," 210–11.
36. Moltmann, *Coming of God*, 6.

must not identify the coming kingdom with any present political or ecclesial power, which leads to oppressive idolatries and messianic violence.[37] Similarly, apocalypticism must not take the form of historical apocalypticism that marks the date of the catastrophic end without hope for creation in the midst of its perishing. Moltmann quotes Martin Luther's claim that, if he thought the world was going to end tomorrow, he would plant a tree today.[38] That is the distinction between an historical apocalyptic that sees only the end of the world, and an eschatological apocalyptic that sees in the end the new beginning for all creation. Both historical millenarianism and historical apocalypticism transpose eschatology into time and thus distort it.

The second distortion of eschatology, transposing eschatology into eternity, Moltmann also refers to as "presentative" eschatologies or eschatologies of the "eternal present."[39] He sees this in the early Barth, Bultmann, and Tillich, with roots going back at least to Schleiermacher. In this vision, eschatology refers to the ever-present possibility for the in-breaking of the eternal in the present moment. Time flows on as it will, marking merely the transience and the natural cycles of life. What is redemptive is not the flow of time, but the possibility in this moment—in *any* moment—of encountering and deciding for the eternal. Moltmann notes Barth's use of metaphors:

> Even his [Barth's] own metaphors betray this: the image of the overhanging rock-face which he uses for eternity points to the limit and end of the way, and if "every wave of time breaks on the shore of eternity," we no longer have to do with a river, not even with a "river of time." We are then dealing with the eternal return of the same thing, in the tides, with their ebb and flow.[40]

Moltmann is troubled by Barth's apparent acquiescence to a naturalistic understanding of time, time as transience, time as perpetual perishing. This natural (and to his mind, moribund) understanding of time is closer to the "blithe resignation" of Ecclesiastes than the "messianic passion" of Isaiah.[41] Such an understanding of time is more reflective of the unfolding, evolving, chthonic cycles of nature. It is time as *chronos*, consuming all its children.

---

37. Ibid., 192.
38. Ibid., 235.
39. Ibid., 26.
40. Ibid., 19.
41. Ibid.

"The reduction of eschatology to time . . . abolishes eschatology altogether, subjecting it to *chronos*, the power of transience."[42]

We can debate to what extent this is an accurate read of the early Barth, Bultmann, and Tillich. Moltmann notes that the later Barth moves away from this position, but never fully repudiates it. It is not insignificant that, with regard to Schleiermacher, Moltmann quotes from his *Speeches On Religion* rather than his *Glaubenslehre*, a curious choice if he is considering Schleiermacher's theological (rather than his "apologetic") thinking. He also dismisses Schleiermacher's perspective, and the presentative perspective more broadly, as "mysticism," as if calling it "mysticism" were a self-evident refutation. Moltmann cannot quite shake a latent suspicion of anything "mystical" that characterized his earlier work and much of Reformed theology. "The flower garden of irrational mysticism spreads out on the soil of rationalistic enlightenment."[43]

In any case, Moltmann is concerned that these presentative eschatologies ultimately are devoid of hope for suffering creation. The human creature may find redemption in the possibility of eternal communion present in every moment, but the rest of creation is seemingly only the condition of possibility for that communion, the stage on which the drama plays out. Nature drops out of the narrative. Yet Romans 8:18ff—a crucial text for Moltmann—clearly enfolds the suffering of the whole creation within the promise of future liberation.

Thus both distortions of eschatology—transposing eschatology into time and transposing eschatology into eternity—fail to address the crises of creation in their interconnected complexity. "Today, exploitation, oppression, alienation, the destruction of nature, and inner despair make up the vicious circle in which we are killing ourselves and our world."[44]

Christian eschatology refers neither to the future of time nor to the timeless presence of eternity. It refers rather to the new creation, a new creation that does not simply emerge out of past and present possibilities, but is rather the advent of the *novum*, the new—a newness, however, that gathers up and recreates the old rather than discarding it.[45] For Moltmann, nothing astonishingly new emerges out of the past and the present (a debatable claim given what we know about evolution and emergence); the truly

42. Ibid., 13.
43. Moltmann, *Man*, 35.
44. Moltmann, *Future of Creation*, 110.
45. Moltmann, *Coming of God*, 27–29.

new comes from the future. Christ's resurrection is the ultimate *novum*, emerging not out of possibilities latent in the past or the present, but from a radical advent of new life from God's future. In the resurrection, the line of causality, the line so carefully mapped out by scientists, is broken.

Moltmann is very careful to affirm that the old is not obliterated, but rather gathered up or recreated in the new. *Contra* Marcion's *Deus novus*, the God of creation and redemption is faithful to the beautiful and broken creation that groans for redemption; it will be taken up and made new.[46] Of course this new creation will be (indeed, *must* be) free from the power of *chronos*—"death will be no more, mourning and crying and pain will be no more, for the first things have passed away" (Rev. 21:4b)—so the recreation is also a sieving, with the seeming negativities of the old creation strained out from the new. But exactly what constitutes detritus and what good creation is a contested question.

Moltmann traces his eschatological vision as three nested concentric circles, from the least inclusive (but first experienced) to the most inclusive: personal eschatology, historical eschatology, and cosmic eschatology. He argues that the cosmic can include the personal and the historical, but not the other way around.[47] Thus it is an error to make personal eschatology the center of eschatological reflection (as much popular piety does), as it risks excluding the historical and cosmic dimensions, which are in fact the condition of possibility for the personal in the first place. Of course, it could be argued that the cosmic, far from including the historical and the personal, actually swallows them up in its vast reaches of space and time. "What are human beings, that you are mindful of them?" (Ps. 8:4a). Here is the "infinite immensity" that so terrified Pascal. Can the cosmic dimension have an enduring place in an eschatological schema that so privileges the personal?

Moltmann rejects personal eschatologies that posit an understanding of life after death that robs this life of meaning: "better to love life here and now as unreservedly as if death really were 'the finish.'"[48] On the other hand, the denial of life after death can be just as destructive as distorted affirmations of life after death. If a "life-denying" vision of life after death is a "religious fraud," so there is an "irreligious fraud," namely, the fear of death that causes us to suppress the awareness of death: "suppressed awareness of

---

46. Ibid., 29.
47. Ibid., 131–32.
48. Ibid., 50.

death buries us alive."[49] Neither the denial of death nor the suppression of death permits the full flowering of love. "Love lets us experience the livingness of life and the deadliness of death."[50] To suppress death is to suppress love (which causes one to ponder: does a new creation where "death is no more" thereby suffer a diminishment of love?). For Moltmann, both the fear of death and the suppression of death constrict life, whereas trust in eternal life enables us to dwell in and with other creatures in compassion and peace.

The way we envision this eternal life is crucial. Moltmann insists that the Christian hope is not for the immortality of the soul; it is rather hope for the resurrection of the flesh—all flesh, not just human flesh. God does not desire to be in relation only with "parts" of the human being (the human soul), but rather with the whole human being, flesh and soul. And this holism extends beyond the individual human being. We are defined by our relations, our social contexts, our histories, our ecologies. Only through the restoration of all things, the redemption of all flesh, can God's love for the individual be fully realized.

Moltmann notes the ambiguity in the Christian tradition with regard to death (a point that Kathryn Tanner explores as well, below). Death is seen both as the result of original sin and as the natural end of the finite creature. Moltmann leans toward the latter understanding, but he situates it within his eschatological vision, so that death is a part of the frail and finite creation that will be overcome in the new creation. Nature is "fallen" in the sense that it is incomplete, an as yet unfulfilled promise. Death may not always be the ruinous result of sin; it is possible to have a natural death rather than a "sinner's death."[51] Nevertheless all death is a transient aspect of a creation yearning for eschatological fulfillment. In the new creation, death will be no more. Death and the frailty of creaturely becoming are the occasion for sin (a "detonator" waiting to go off, as Moltmann puts it[52]), and so sin would continue to stalk the new creation if death were not swallowed up forever.

However, this deathless new creation is not a transhistorical, otherworldly realm. It is the new creation of *this* world, a transformation (completion, not dissolution) of this time and this space. This is critical

49. Ibid., 51.
50. Ibid., 55.
51. Ibid., 89.
52. Ibid., 91.

for Moltmann because transposing eschatology into eternity risks "leaving behind" much of the good creation that yearns for redemption. Moltmann is troubled by the reality of so many creatures failing to achieve the fulfillment appropriate to their modes of being (such as the "pelican chick," below). So many lives (human and other-than-human) are cut short, unfulfilled, incomplete. The claim that "my soul goes to heaven when I die" is a mockery of a creation so full of suffering. A new creation must include space and time and strength for further growth and becoming—yet without the attendant suffering and death.[53] "This of course means thinking of change without transience, time without the past, and life without death."[54] Whether this is indeed possible, or even conceivable, is unclear.

Moltmann argues that, without cosmic eschatology, Christianity inevitably becomes gnostic, envisioning redemption as *from* the world and the body rather than *of* the world and the body.[55] There is what Moltmann considers an unfaithful tendency in some trajectories of Christian theology to leave this world and this body behind. But, as McDougall summarizes Moltmann: "at every stage of the messianic history of God with the world—in creation, redemption, and glorification—*embodiment* is the goal of God's works."[56] This emphasis on embodiment provides another point of contact with the work of Sallie McFague in the next chapter.

Moltmann sees in eschatological visions of the annihilation of the cosmos (which he associates with later Lutheran orthodoxy, though not with Luther himself) an overemphasis on a theology of the cross and an insufficiently incarnational theology.[57] He sees in eschatological visions of the divinization of the cosmos (which he associates with Eastern Orthodox traditions) an overemphasis on a theology of glory. The Calvinist eschatological vision of the transformation of the cosmos could be a mediating position, but Moltmann critiques it as being insufficiently radical, focusing on the transformation of the *form* of the world rather than its *substance*.

> If the new creation is to be an imperishable and eternal creation,
> it must be new not only over against the world of sin and death,

---

53. Ibid., 118.
54. Moltmann, *God in Creation*, 213
55. Moltmann, *Coming of God*, 259.
56. McDougall, *Pilgrimage of Love*, 117 (my emphasis).
57. Moltmann, *Coming of God*, 268.

but over against the first, temporal creation too. The substantial conditions of creaturely existence itself must be changed.[58]

Moltmann also rejects ecofeminist approaches, for, while he is sympathetic with the desire to affirm the goodness of embodied, earthly existence, he argues that too often hope is truncated to fit within the confines of nature as we have it, but nature as we have it is neither the original good creation nor the new creation, but rather the "fallen" creation yearning for fulfillment.[59] As he says, with perhaps a touch of scorn:

> Deep respect for "the good earth" does not mean that we have to give ourselves up for burial with the consolation that we shall live on in worms and plants. It means waiting for the day when the earth will open, the dead will rise, and the earth together with these dead will "be raised" for its new creation.[60]

Moltmann's hope for cosmic redemption can be traced through three symbols: sabbath, Shekinah, and the heavenly Jerusalem. He notes that in the Genesis creation narrative, everything is created in dualities except for the sabbath. Thus the sabbath awaits its partner, the *Shekinah* of God, in eschatological glory.[61] The sabbath is God's exile in and with creation awaiting final reunion with God's coming glory (*Shekinah*), in which all creation will glorify God. All creation is a wandering Aramean (Deut 26:5) on a journey with and toward God, weaving together sabbath and *Shekinah*, space and time, heaven and earth. The symbol of that final meeting is the heavenly Jerusalem, the city of God. The heavenly Jerusalem represents for Moltmann the final consummation of history between human beings and creation. The garden in the city is the symbol of the perfect harmonization between civilization and nature.[62] Unlike Moltmann's theological methodology, this garden is quite tame. There will be no death in the heavenly Jerusalem, *chronos* enjoys no more efficacy, "for the first things have passed away."

However, lest one take in this vision with an eye fixed too narrowly on the joy of the heavenly Jerusalem for human beings, Moltmann reminds us that the last word must be the glorification of God. He draws on Augustine's

---

58. Ibid., 272.

59. This is a critique that has dogged Moltmann since his earliest work: the question of the absolute or relative worth of nature. See for example Philip Hefner, "The Future as Our Future."

60. Moltmann, *Coming of God*, 277.

61. Ibid., 283.

62. Ibid., 314–15.

distinction between sinners, who "make use" of God in order to "enjoy" the world, and believers, who "make use" of the world in order to "enjoy" God.[63] Moltmann echoes Calvinist orthodoxy: the chief end of human creatures is to glorify God and enjoy God forever. This glorification does not nullify or supersede but rather "gathers up" and "perfects" all our strivings in the "aesthetic experience of doxology."[64] The end is joy, the joy of creatures to be sure, but most essentially the joy of God. Creation is divine play, divine fantasy, the outflowing of God's creative imagination. As play, it serves no other final purpose than joy. "It is like a great song or a splendid poem or a wonderful dance of his fantasy, for the communication of his divine plenitude. The laughter of the universe is God's delight. It is the universal Easter laughter."[65]

There is a creative unruliness to Moltmann's vision; as I have said, it is a profusion of imaginative wagers, creative excurses, and passionate proposals. In order to cast his vision into sharper relief, I want to consider briefly four additional contemporary thinkers, each of whom is working at the dynamic tension between a hopeful orientation toward the future and a humble cherishing of the good green earth. Each thinker resolves that tension in different ways. These four eschatological snapshots further map out the eschatological landscape and help us to locate Moltmann within it.

Evolution and Spiritualization: Pierre Teilhard de Chardin

In *The Human Phenomenon* Pierre Teilhard de Chardin endeavors to transform the way human beings *see*. To fail to see properly, he argues, is to miss the divine call to participate in the grand process of the "spiritualization" of the universe. Human beings see lifeless matter and alienated spirit; they see conflict between materialism and spiritualism. But Teilhard wants human beings to see that spirit is seeded in matter, that matter is merely the outside of things, while spirit is the inside of things. Everything has a physical and a psychic dimension. Tangential energy (studied by science) connects everything with everything else on its own level, but radial energy (the real focus of Teilhard's thinking) draws everything upward toward greater complexity and consciousness, toward the emergence of spirit. To see this emergence is to become a part of the ultimate adventure, binding our energy to the

63. Ibid., 323.
64. Ibid., 324.
65. Ibid., 339.

evolutionary process as we draw ever closer to the animating center of all things. To see this emergence is to see the providence of God at work in the world, and to participate in it.

Teilhard argues that complexity and consciousness are connected and emerge in tandem. Both are seeded throughout matter. Life presumes pre-life: this prelife may be miniscule in some cases but it never recedes to the vanishing point. Complexity-consciousness is incipient in all things, and it reaches its culmination in the personalizing force of hominization or humanization. This force (seen most clearly in human beings) seeks unification (moving beyond individual and tribal limits), centration (the intensification of reflective consciousness), and spiritualization (the upward impulse toward the Omega Point).[66] The evolutionary process of the emergence of complexity-consciousness and the personalizing force of hominization leads the universe through the stages of cosmogenesis (the emergence of the inorganic world), biogenesis (the emergence of life), anthropogenesis (the emergence of human thought), and noogenesis (humanization, thought, and love encircling the globe).[67] The final stage of universal evolution, and the animating center that pulls all things along the lines of radial energy toward their final fulfillment, is the Omega Point, which Teilhard also identifies with the Cosmic Christ. The Cosmic Christ is the ultimate personalization and hominization of the universe.

Teilhard is something of a patron saint in ecological theology, and not without reason. His emphasis on an evolving world and the critical role humans may play in such a world (for good or ill—though he thought more often good than ill); his affirmation of the interconnectedness of all things not only through tangential energy but especially through the radial energy that draws all things upward; his vision of the universe, not as a lifeless shell to be cracked open by scientists but rather as a living reality full of mystery and meaning—all these are important dimensions of an ecological orientation.

However, many aspects of Teilhard's vision are troubling. No doubt he drank deeply from the wells of progressive optimism in his time, so he can perhaps be excused for his exuberant call for human beings to "build the earth."[68] And he was aware that change and suffering are the inevitable by-products of a universe where the plurality of matter can resist the unity

---

66. Teilhard de Chardin, *Human Phenomenon*, 216–23.
67. Ibid., 130–47.
68. Teilhard de Chardin, *Building the Earth*.

of spirit; he was not exactly a Pollyanna.[69] Nevertheless, he had little doubt as to the directionality of the universe—and it is rather strikingly anthropocentric for an ecological vision. Personalization and hominization: this is the ultimate destiny of the universe. Or, rather, the penultimate destiny. The ultimate destiny is the full spiritualization of the universe, when all things become one in the Cosmic Christ. But the fate of matter in this ultimate destiny is ambiguous. At times Teilhard seems to view matter as a kind of stage rocket, essential in providing lift for spirituality, but ultimately falling away and burning up in the atmosphere while spirit continues its journey toward the Omega Point. For example: "The end of the world: the reversal of equilibrium, detaching the spirit, complete at last, from its material matrix, to rest now with its full weight on God-Omega."[70]

It is this dualistic ambiguity in Teilhard that makes tenuous the hopefulness of his vision. On the one hand, he clearly affirms a directionality to the evolutionary process: evolution is moving toward ever-greater complexity and consciousness. He intended this to be a scientific, not simply a theological, claim. At the same time, once spirit has truly emerged into consciousness in human beings, Teilhard all but loses interest in ongoing evolution in a material sense. Now the focus is on spiritualization, on radial energy, on noogenesis. Whether or not evolution in a material sense is ongoing becomes less significant. In fact, given that physical reality ultimately will be consumed in the ecstatic union of spiritualization and the Cosmic Christ, ongoing material evolution is functionally irrelevant. Of course Teilhard uses the term "evolution" to refer to this whole physical and spiritual process, so the ongoing personalization of creation through human beings is just as much evolution for Teilhard as neo-Darwinian evolution. However, it is fair to say that most scientists would not recognize what Teilhard is talking about as evolution, at least once it moves beyond the level of tangential energy.

Teilhard's evolutionary dynamism and his affirmation of the material world without succumbing to materialism—these trajectories find their echo in Moltmann. But Teilhard's vision drinks too deeply from the wells of technological and scientific progressivism, and his ultimate vision of material reality falling away into nothingness, having achieved its purpose in providing "lift" for the spiritual, is marred by a residual Cartesian dualism that runs contrary to Moltmann's holistic vision of a new creation. A vision

---

69. See Teilhard de Chardin, *Human Phenomenon*, 224–26.
70. Ibid., 206.

which sees matter as something ultimately to be cast away cannot fuel hope for an incarnate future. For Moltmann, a Christian hope must be hope for the transformation of all things—for the spirit *and* for the material matrix in which it is embedded—or it is not hope at all.

Breaking the Evolutionary Line: Christopher Southgate

Compared to Teilhard, Christopher Southgate has a far keener sense of the waste and loss that is endemic to the evolutionary process. In *The Groaning of Creation*, he raises the problem of the pelican chick (first articulated by Holmes Rolston and later by Jay McDaniel).[71] The white pelican typically lays two eggs. The second egg, the second chick, is an "insurance" chick, there to step in should something go wrong with the first chick. If the first chick is healthy, it will peck and harass the second chick, denying it food and driving it out of the nest. The second pelican chick almost always dies of starvation or predation. As an evolutionary adaptation, this is successful. If something goes wrong with the first chick, there is a backup. From the outside, this is an efficient system. But from the inside, from the subjective experience of the baby chick, this is tragic. In most cases, this chick is born only to suffer hostility, alienation, starvation, and early death. Whatever opportunities for fulfilling existence there are for the older pelican chick, they are denied the baby. The baby chick is simply a means to an end in the unfolding evolutionary process. But is it an end in itself? Is it an end for God? As Holmes Rolston suggests, "If God watches the sparrow fall, God must do so from a very great distance."[72]

How do we hold together the affirmation of the very goodness of creation with our awareness of the brutality and suffering endemic to the evolutionary process that brought us into being? Southgate wants to affirm that creation is good, not only because God declares it so but also because it is productive of values. We must acknowledge that pain, suffering, and death are endemic to the evolutionary process; however, this process was the only means by which God could have made a world capable of producing the beauty we actually see in creation. Southgate affirms that God suffers with and in creation in the incarnation, that the cross is the great embodiment of divine compassion for the world, and that the resurrection is the inauguration of God's transformation of creation. In this transformed creation,

71. See Rolston, *Science and Religion*, and McDaniel, *Of God and Pelicans*.
72. Rolston, *Science and Religion*, 140.

every creature can and must find fulfillment appropriate to its kind. Thus in the new creation the evolutionary pressures that rendered the pelican chick's life nasty, brutish, and short have been miraculously relieved.

In these affirmations Southgate is circumventing several possibilities that he considers problematic. He rejects the notion of a "fallen creation" as an explanation for suffering both because the seeming negativities of creation (predation, parasitism, suffering, and death) predate the arrival of *Homo sapiens* and because these very negativities are integral to the process by which complexity and beauty emerge. He also rejects a process approach (such as Suchocki's, below), both because he finds it insufficiently faithful to the biblical vision of God and also because it cannot provide the very thing that Southgate considers essential to an evolutionary eschatology: a vision that promises the ultimate redemption and fulfillment of all things, not in a transhistorical otherworldly realm (or even in God) but rather in a re-creation of time and space, that is, in a new creation.

Southgate is more acutely aware than Teilhard of the cruelty, suffering, waste, and loss that are seemingly ineradicable aspects of the evolutionary process, and he does not affirm a positive trajectory to evolutionary processes, as if evolution has some immanent, innate progressive arc. On the other hand, he is far more invested than Teilhard in the transformation of this world, and thus of the evolutionary process. Southgate does not wish to leave nature behind in the ascent to the Cosmic Christ. Redemption must take place in and through the creation, not outside of it.

Thus there is a profound gap in Southgate between what he can affirm about evolutionary processes and what he must affirm about eschatological fulfillment. For him, that gap is filled by the power of God. Evolution does not have an innately progressive arc, but God can bend or break the evolutionary line. The new creation will be the work of God, not an emergent from evolutionary processes. It is not so much an outworking of God's providential care as the advent of God's eschatological future.

Southgate's perspective is deeply shaped by evolutionary biology and the suffering endemic to evolutionary processes. Moltmann shares this perspective, though Southgate focuses with greater intensity on the ways other-than-human creatures are shaped (and misshaped) by the process, while Moltmann tends to focus on the human creature. Southgate occasionally gives way to scientifically informed but rather fantastical speculations—such as the painless, unafraid "dance" of predators and prey in the new creation[73]—of which I suspect Moltmann would be wary. Once the line has been broken, better to draw on imagination and poetry to dare to affirm what the gospel promises than to get bogged down in sorting out energy systems and photosynthetic lions in the new creation. Having said that, many of Southgate's themes—a valuing of creation as incomplete and groaning but not fallen, a longing for a fully embodied new creation with space and time for the full becoming of all creatures—find deep echoes in Moltmann's vision.

Process Hope: Marjorie Suchocki

In *The End of Evil*, Marjorie Suchocki articulates a neo-process eschatology in response to the reality of evil. Process thought has commonly been employed to respond to questions of suffering, but it has been critiqued for being unable to affirm the subjective significance of the individual and the possibility for individual fulfillment. Suchocki wants to respond to that challenge.

She notes two primary trajectories within the Christian tradition with regard to evil: evil as the result of misused freedom (which she traces to Augustine), and evil as the result of finitude (which she traces to Irenaeus). If freedom is the root of evil, if evil is rooted in the subjective will (sin), then the problem of evil can be resolved with a divided eschatology: heaven for the redeemed and hell for the unredeemed. However, if evil is rooted in the objective structures of existence itself, this divided eschatology breaks down, and it risks an eschatology that imagines redemption as the redemption *from* rather than *of* the world.

Suchocki finds in Whitehead and process thought a mediating path between Augustinian subjectivism and Irenaean objectivism. Process thought strongly emphasizes the relationship between finitude and evil. Whitehead refers to perpetual perishing as an evil, that is, the way temporality itself constantly consumes the present: "the ultimate evil in the temporal world is deeper than any specific evil. It lies in the fact that the past fades, that time is a 'perpetual perishing.'"[74] Evil is also located in the loss of possibility that is concomitant with every act of concrescence. To choose one possibility is to reject many other possibilities, and in all of those rejected possibilities much beauty is lost. Even the reality of relationality, so emphasized by pro-

---

73. Southgate, *Groaning of Creation*, 88.
74. Whitehead, *Process and Reality*, 340.

cess thought, is the occasion for evil, as actual occasions have their range of possibilities widened or narrowed by other actual occasions. Finitude is good; temporality is good; freedom and creativity are good; relationality is good—or, at least, these are the conditions of possibility for goodness. But they are also the conditions of possibility for evil. Thus evil is rooted in finitude, in the tragic structure of existence itself.

But process thought emphasizes just as strongly the freedom of each actual occasion—so much so that creativity, rather than being understood as a creation of God, is a metaphysical principle to which both God and the world are bound. No doubt an actual occasion is significantly shaped by the prior actual occasions it has prehended. Nevertheless God offers to each actual occasion graded possibilities, from the highest possible realization of beauty for that actual occasion to lesser instantiations. However, there are situations where the highest possibility for an actual occasion is still evil. But in most cases actual occasions will have some measure of freedom to actualize possibilities of beauty—and to actualize possibilities of evil as well. Thus evil is rooted in freedom as well as finitude.

One common critique of process thought has been that it does not allow for any final hope. The world is coeternal with God, the process goes ever on, the conditions for goodness—and thus for evil—endure forever. Evil can never be overcome within history. The question is, then, are there intimations of a transhistorical order in which evil is overcome? Whitehead already has the notion of objective immortality—that goodness endures not only in the ongoing life of the world but also by becoming a part of the consequent nature of God: God remembers. But Suchocki does not consider this sufficient. She argues that God must feel not only the objectivity of the actual occasion (after its concrescence) but also its subjectivity, its enjoyment of its own moment of becoming.[75]

Significantly, Suchocki does not consider even this affirmation of "subjective immortality" sufficient, because if an actual occasion is immortalized in its moment of becoming, and if that becoming was painful, then its suffering is immortalized. This would be hell, not heaven. Thus Suchocki argues that neither objective immortality nor subjective immortality is sufficient. We must imagine that there is space and time within God in which

---

75. There are some tensions here with Whitehead's insistence that an actual occasion in the moment of its becoming is private and inviolable, but tracing these out would drag us into an intra-process debate that is far afield.

creatures can find the fulfillment appropriate to their kind that they were denied in this life.

There is a process dimension to Moltmann's vision. He does not explicitly draw on the metaphysical categories of Whitehead, but more broadly he affirms the interiority of creatures, both their dependence and their freedom to become, conjoined with a divine openness to the world and the suffering that is concomitant with such openness. But process thought is significantly shaped by the awareness of the tragic dimension of existence, and while Moltmann certainly shares that awareness, it is precisely that tragic dimension that will be subsumed within the comedic vision of a new creation. Suchocki's affirmation of the need for space and time within God for creatures to find their fulfillment is a step closer to Moltmann's perspective, but what could it mean for a creature to have space and time for becoming apart from the creation that is the very context of creaturely becoming? For Moltmann creatures need a new creation, one that has been redeemed from its tragic structure, to find the fulfillment appropriate to their kind, and Suchocki's vision cannot offer that.

Eschatology for a World That Ends: Kathryn Tanner

In *Jesus, Humanity, and the Kingdom*, Kathryn Tanner articulates an eschatology for a "world that ends." She takes for granted a scientific account of the world which not only assures us that every living thing will die but also suggests the likelihood that all living things will die (even if in billions of years). Tanner considers the debate between the "big crunch" and an "infinite expansion" to be undecided. More recent research points to the latter future, that is, the infinite expansion of the universe—everything flying away from everything else at an ever-increasing speed—suggesting that the future of the universe is cold, dark, lonely, and dead. Closer to home, our sun will burn up one day, shutting down all the life processes on this planet. Of course we may beat the sun to it through ecological or nuclear catastrophe. Tanner argues for a theological vision that can endure even in the face of such endings.

Tanner notes that one strategy in response to this is to question the scientific assumptions of the end, not on scientific grounds but on theological grounds. We see this with Southgate above (and of course with Moltmann more generally). Science can only draw a line from where we are to where we may be based on immanent forces and factors. But can God not bend or break that line? Such thinkers could point to the resurrection of Jesus as paradigmatic. Science could never draw the line from Jesus' corpse to an empty tomb; God broke in to the immanent processes with a new possibility, a new reality. And if God can raise Jesus from the dead, then God can break any other line of causality. According to this line of thought, the scientific vision of a world that ends does not take sufficient account of the power of God. Despite what scientists say, God can create a new future that is life, not death, and even a new creation where death and suffering will be no more.

However, Tanner wants to consider another possibility: that Christian eschatology could be articulated in such a way as to be compatible with any scientific vision for the end of things. Does eschatology have a stake in whether or not the world will come to an end? She draws a parallel line to developments in theologies of creation. Schleiermacher, for example, argued (as Aquinas had before him) that the doctrine of creation points to the absolute dependence of everything on God. This relationship of absolute dependence obtains whether or not creation had a beginning in time, or time began with creation, or creation is eternal. In other words, the doctrine of creation is independent of any claim as to the beginning of creation. Schleiermacher will leave it to science to determine whether and how the universe began. The theological affirmation of the absolute dependence of all things on God remains, regardless of how science solves the puzzle of beginnings.

Tanner argues for a similar development in eschatological thinking, that is, to formulate an eschatological vision in such a way that it is independent of developments of science with regard to the end of the world or the directionality of evolution. The Christian theologian should not have to wait on pins and needles for the latest deliverances of science before she or he can make a theological claim. At the same time, eschatological affirmations should not stand in direct contradiction to scientific determinations of the end (as they appear to with Southgate). Given the scientific consensus that the world will end, one way or another, Tanner argues that theologians need to contemplate an eschatology that can make sense of the "failure of the world."

For Tanner such an eschatology could still be focused on this world (as opposed to escapist and otherworldly) and cosmic in scope (as opposed to anthropocentric and individualistic), but it would have to mitigate its future orientation. The promise of eschatological consummation would refer, not to a future state toward which the world moves, but rather to possibilities for new dimensions of relationality to the triune God here and now. Eternal life is a present reality in union with Christ; it is not directly tied to the future (or lack of future) of the world. Ultimately it is not particularly tied to any mode of time. Tanner imagines eschatology in spatial rather than temporal metaphors: we live in God.[76]

This is not to say that eschatology is fully realized, for "life in God" stands in contestation with the "realm of death," with death understood in the broadest (biblical) sense as all that cuts us off from communion with others and with God. There is "more to come" in eternal life, both in terms of the constant reshaping of this world to better reflect the reality of "life in God" and also in the possibility of future consummation with God (independent of the "scientific" future of the world). Nevertheless, we live in God now, not in some eschatological future.

Contra Southgate, Tanner's eschatology does not entail the elimination of death. She acknowledges the distinction between "good" death and "bad" death, with bad death entailing the affliction (rather than simply the end) of the finite creature.[77] Death can be too soon, too painful, too disruptive of communion; it can take the form of alienating disease or debilitating poverty or being cut off from community. The Christian is called to resist death in these senses. The promise of "life in God" stands in judgment on the realm of (bad) death. But death as finitude need not be bad. It is the natural end of the temporal life of the finite creature. In life, in death, in life-beyond-death, the creature remains in God eternally.

Hope, then, does not come from the future (which may or may not progress and may or may not come to an end), but rather from the fact that all of creation lives in God. No doubt this claim stands in tension with a world stalked by affliction, the world as the realm of death. We are called to contest this realm of death with the good news of life in God. There is work to be done in our struggles against the death-dealing powers. But ultimately the death-dealing powers are already overcome because we live in God. As Luther's famous hymn has it, their doom is sure—not because in some imagined future they will finally irrevocably be defeated but rather because they have always already been defeated.

Moltmann shares Tanner's nuanced understanding of death in the biblical tradition, and would certainly echo the call to resist "bad" death

---

76. Tanner, *Jesus, Humanity, and the Trinity*, 104.
77. Ibid., 105.

on behalf of the God of life. However, I suspect he would consider this an "interim perspective," a Holy Saturday perspective. The fullness of Christian hope for Moltmann is not simply the elimination of "bad" death and the consent to "good" death but rather the swallowing up of death itself (Isa 25:8). In the end Tanner would likely fall prey to the critique Moltmann makes of Barth, that in her vision the kingdom comes from heaven to earth rather than from the future to the present, or to quote Paul Althaus, that "we arrive at the completion [of history] not by traversing the longitudinal lines of history to their end, but by erecting everywhere in history the perpendicular line."[78] In other words, Tanner is transposing eschatology into eternity; hers is a "presentative" eschatology. Shorn from the power of God's future, historical and material possibilities are ultimately left behind rather than redeemed in such a vision.

Moltmann's eschatological vision has a vast sweep, and he endeavors to inscribe nature within that vision at every turn. However, despite his theocentric reflections on the glory of God, ultimately his vision cannot quite escape the gravitational pull of anthropocentrism (or "theanthropocentrism"). It cannot be insignificant that Moltmann's final eschatological vision is a city. (Granted he is following a [not *the*] scriptural trajectory with this.) But note that the vision of the heavenly Jerusalem is the conclusion of his discussion of *cosmic* eschatology. We might expect the city to be the apotheosis of human historical existence, but of cosmic existence? Is the whole purpose of the cosmos the provision of a habitable environment for the human creature?

Moltmann makes space for nature in the new creation, but it is human space (city-space). Note that nature exists in the eschaton only as a garden, a symbol of the human cultivation of nature. This seems to be the nineteenth-century dream of progress, humanity conquering nature, only in a new key. The wilderness, where nature dwells in and for itself (and God), is no more. Nature endures now only as a human construct. Thus we see that, despite Moltmann's consistent efforts to hold nature within the narrative of redemption, what we actually find there is a denatured nature, a humanized nature.

Moltmann's theological vision has tremendous breadth and depth; it is generative of both profound insights and unsettling questions. My reading

---

78. Quoted in Moltmann, *Coming of God*, 16.

of Moltmann has been focused primarily on two particular threads: hope in an open future grounded in divine creativity, and solidarity with a beautiful and fragile creation. Or again, how does one articulate an incarnate hope, a hope that encompasses all things without doing violence to their fragile particularities? How does one envision a restoration of all things that does not obliterate apparent negativities that may in fact be the *sine qua non* of a good and evolving creation?

I have observed that, despite concerted efforts to the contrary, nature as nature ultimately drops out of Moltmann's eschatological vision. The anthropocentrism endemic to the narrative of redemption only permits space for nature insofar as it has been humanized. In the new creation, there is a garden, not a wilderness. The seeming negativities of nature (competition, predation, parasitism, suffering, death) are seen by Moltmann to be, if not quite distortions of nature as it was created to be, then signs of its incompleteness, its groaning for redemption. In the new creation, these negativities will be no more. The lion will eat straw like the ox—but is this still a lion?

Moltmann wants to insist that there must be space and time for further becoming, but without suffering and death. Yet everything we know about creaturely becoming has been formed in the crucible of evolutionary pressures. What is creaturely becoming apart from suffering? If love and death are intertwined, as Moltmann suggests, what is love in a deathless new creation?

In Job 38–40 the God of the whirlwind sings of the wild fecundity and fierceness of creation, rhapsodizing ecstatically of Behemoth ("the first of the great acts of God") and Leviathan ("were not even the gods overwhelmed at the sight of it?"), of the springs of the sea and the recesses of the deep, of snow and rain and dew and stars, of ravenous lions and calving mountain goats and the ostrich's plumage and the horse's strength. On and on it goes like this, page after page, amazing, wild, rapturous language about the terrible beauty of creation. Instead of a preserve of nature in the midst of human meaning (a garden), the God of the whirlwind imagines a preserve of human meaning in the midst of a teeming and buzzing cacophony of other creatures. The human animal has its time and place, but no more. At the end of Moltmann's eschatology there is Easter laughter, to be sure, but the God of the whirlwind has been silenced.

How does one articulate an incarnate hope, a hope that encompasses all things, without doing violence to their fragile particularities? How does one envision a restoration of all things that does not obliterate apparent negativities which may in fact be the *sine qua non* of a good and evolving creation? As I have said, Moltmann walks the fault line between a hopeful orientation toward the future and a humble cherishing of the good, green earth. However, despite his passionate and commendable efforts to preserve the many beautiful and broken creatures of the earth, they are ultimately swallowed up—redeemed, yes, but denatured—by an eschatological vision that cannot finally give space to the tragic, the wild, the other-than-human. Moltmann's vision of the heavenly Jerusalem is ardently hopeful, but its reach finally fails to extend to the whole of creation. Much of the good, green earth—the beautiful and broken creation to which we are called to consent with humility—cannot pass through the gate.

3

Subjunctive Faith
Humility and Hope in Sallie McFague

No one has labored at the nexus of theology and ecology more tirelessly than Sallie McFague. From her early reflections on religious language and the promise of a metaphorical approach to theology to her development of the model of the world as God's body and her explorations of spirituality and economics—through all of this McFague has consistently placed her constructive, imaginative proposals in the service of liberative praxis on behalf of a suffering creation and a warming world.

In the previous chapter I asked, how does one articulate an incarnate hope, a hope that encompasses all things, without doing violence to their fragile particularities? How does one envision a restoration of all things that does not obliterate apparent negativities that may in fact be the *sine qua non* of a good and evolving creation? My judgment was that Jürgen Moltmann walks the fault line between a hopeful orientation to the future and a humble cherishing of the good, green earth—but that ultimately, despite his passionate efforts to the contrary, nature *as nature* is lost in his vision. The passionate hopefulness of his vision is incontrovertible, and precisely because of that, in the end he cannot humbly consent to a tragically structured creation.

The same question hovers over this chapter, but from the opposite direction. McFague is particularly troubled by the destructive potential of much Christian theology, its hierarchical dualism, its tacit or explicit underwriting of domination systems, its tendency to obliterate the many beautiful and broken creatures of the earth in service to a monarchial model of God wed to a rapacious economic system. In the midst of this,

McFague will stand in solidarity with the earth. She resists the anthropocentric drift of much Christian theology. She rejects any vision in which creation is merely a stage for the divine-human drama of salvation to play out or a vast store of resources to be violently exploited at human whims to serve solely human ends. McFague is willing to revision or even abandon classical theological claims in order to preserve the enduring value of a suffering creation. Her vision will not allow an all-consuming theology (even a passionately hopeful eschatology) to subsume (and thereby obliterate) nature in all its tragic beauty.

However, as with Moltmann, McFague understands hope to be vital to liberative praxis. And how could it be otherwise? Despair is more likely to engender benign indifference, nihilistic abandon, or violent resentment than passionate action on behalf of those who suffer. As with Moltmann, McFague locates this vital hope in the power of God. But for McFague, that power appears to be limited to the "if only" of human reciprocity. That is, God's power is a resource available to human beings *if only* they will draw on it for the healing of the world. This "subjunctive faith" may be seen as deeply empowering of the human creature. There will be no *deus ex machina*, no unilateral divine rescue mission on our behalf. The future is in our hands. As the saying goes, we are the ones we've been waiting for. But if our hope for the future is ultimately grounded not in divine creativity, but in human consent to divine creativity, then that hope becomes tenuous. It is difficult to sustain a subjunctive faith in the midst of rapidly deteriorating ecosystems, a pathological indifference among the political class, and a willful ignorance among the general public. If hope is ultimately contingent upon human action, is that hope at all?

In what follows I will first consider McFague's theological methodology. I devote more time to this with McFague than I did with Moltmann because McFague makes method itself an object of theological reflection and because her methodology is a significant contribution to theological discourse in its own right. Next I will turn to McFague's central metaphorical venture—the world as God's body—to explore the opportunities and challenges that such an approach brings to an ecological theology. Finally I consider McFague's eschatology proper. Unlike Moltmann, McFague does not place eschatology at the center of her theological reflection, so I will have to stitch her vision together from disparate and at times contradictory fragments.

Throughout I will be exploring the possibilities and limitations of McFague's vision. She is passionately committed to solidarity with the good, green earth. This is the humble dimension of her vision. There is a strong current of consent to the beautiful, fragile, and tragic creation, though this current stands in some tension with the more passionately hopeful strains of her eschatology. However, her vision of hope, even when energized by the narrative of resurrection, is ultimately curtailed by human powers and possibilities. It is a subjunctive vision, an "if only" vision. The question is, does such a vision finally engender—or endanger—hope?

Liberating Metaphors: McFague's Methodology

Arguably McFague's greatest contribution to theological discourse is not her specific doctrinal proposals but her advocacy for a metaphorical approach to theological language. This metaphorical approach can make her difficult to pin down at times. Perhaps like any good theologian, she is always on the move. As Heraclitus said, you cannot step into the same (theological) river twice. This is particularly true in McFague's case, as she sees theology as an ongoing experiment, and she values the playful, protean potential of metaphorical language.

This does not mean that her theology is incoherent. As she maps out her own journey:

> *Metaphorical Theology* laid the groundwork with the claim that since all religious language is metaphorical, alternatives to traditional metaphors are possible. *Models of God* experimented with several alternative models: God as mother, lover, and friend and the world as God's body. *The Body of God* attempted a systematic theology through the lens of one of these models. The present book *[Super, Natural Christians]* suggests that Christian nature spirituality should be based on a subject-subjects model of being, knowing, and doing in place of the subject-object model of Western culture.[1]

This quote reveals the interconnection and evolution of her thought. It also reveals the way the mutability of her metaphorical approach makes it difficult to give a definitive statement of her theology. To McFague's autobiographical mapping we will need to add her later book, *Life Abundant*, which further reshapes and refines her methodology.

---

1. McFague, *Super, Natural Christians*, 2.

Terrence Reynolds helpfully situates McFague's work within a debate between Sheila Greeve Davaney and Carol Christ on historicism and realism in feminist theological discourse.[2] Davaney criticizes several prominent feminist thinkers for methodological inconsistency.[3] On the one hand they make use of a historicist[4] perspective to dismantle patriarchal systems; on the other hand they search for ahistorical foundations for their own constructive alternatives. Feminist thinkers need to be more explicit in naming the relativity of their own constructions and the impossibility of ontological truth. Davaney argues that:

> Theology when viewed in this manner, is a thoroughly human enterprise carried out for human purposes . . . . It seeks, through the critical and creative capacities of the human imagination, to contribute to the construction of interpretive worlds through which human beings can gain orientation in life and thereby pursue sustainable and humane forms of existence.[5]

Thus Davaney advocates for an explicitly historicist, non-realist, constructivist approach with a pragmatic and ethical orientation.

Christ agrees with Davaney that it is important to recognize the historicity of all truth claims and to question any universal claim to ontological reality.[6] Theology is necessarily entangled in a diversity of perspectives and social locations. But the claim that there is no neutral ground from which to make ontological claims does not for Christ mean that we must abandon all truth claims. She criticizes Davaney's vision for theology: "its intellectual detachment, its side-stepping of the question of the referential nature of religious symbols in the lives of those for whom they have meaning, is its greatest weakness, and is a characteristic feminist theologians would do well not to emulate."[7] Feminist theology cannot adopt Davaney's nihilistic and relativistic approach because it violates the truth of experience.

> We acknowledge the perspectival nature of all truth claims, but we are not thoroughgoing relativists, because our feminist experience

2. Reynolds, "Two McFagues."
3. Davaney, "Problems With Feminist Theory."
4. Historicism has a range of meanings. I follow Davaney in using "historicism" to denote a perspective that denies all forms of foundationalism, realism, and the transcendentalized subject.
5. Quoted in Reynolds, "Two McFagues," 291.
6. Christ, "Embodied Thinking."
7. Quoted in Reynolds, "Two McFagues," 293.

> contradicts that. We are not nihilists, because we believe that feminism has the potential to better the world. Similarly, as theologians, we have religious experience and vision which ground our symbols and theological visions . . . . We do experience ourselves and our visions as rooted in being and truth.[8]

Theology may be construction, but constructions do not refer exhaustively to the convictions of the theologian. Though grounded in the vision of the theologian, theological claims are intended to refer to transcendent reality. They may refer imperfectly, but the theological claim is that they do refer. Christ agrees with Davaney that theological claims have pragmatic justifications—"sustainable and humane forms of existence"—but this is not their only justification. They are also justified by their power to give voice to the experiences of those who claim them and to make coherent a broad range of experience.

Davaney and Christ articulate different visions for theological discourse. Davaney embraces a historicist account in which theological language is construction all the way down and theological truth is determined, not as reference to some transcendent reality, but rather through its pragmatic capacity to underwrite humane living. Christ agrees with Davaney's assessment of the fragile and contextual character of theological language, but she holds that it nevertheless does refer, however imperfectly, to a transcendent other. Truth will always be bound by cultural-linguistic context, and there is no "God's eye" perspective from which it may be finally adjudicated; in this Christ agrees with Davaney. Nevertheless the experience of life and faith grounds theological truth claims as much as pragmatic and instrumental considerations.

These considerations are helpful because, as Reynolds argues, McFague pulls both in Davaney's and in Christ's direction at different times in different contexts. On the one hand McFague can be read as in agreement with Davaney. She certainly shares Davaney's understanding of theological discourse as humanly constructed, as bound by historical and cultural-linguistic context. She emphasizes the imaginative, playful role of metaphorical theological language, and is reluctant to suggest that her metaphorical proposals make any ontological claims. In one of her early discussions of the model of the world as God's body, for example, she writes: "we are not slipping back into a search for unmediated divine presence (which the deconstructionists have criticized so thoroughly). There is no way behind this

8. Ibid.

metaphor or any other construal of the God-world relationship."[9] In this seeming rejection of referential truth claims McFague echoes Davaney.

However, in other places McFague seems to echo Christ over against Davaney. McFague is somewhat slippery on this point, to be sure, but she does leave space for (modest) ontological truth claims (insofar as any ontological claim can be said to be modest). As Reynolds points out, McFague speaks of metaphorical theology as "'*mainly* fiction,' '*mainly* elaboration,' '*more* nonsense than truth,' historically conditioned, and able to 'advance *few* solid claims in its behalf.'"[10] Needless to say, discourse of "mainly" and "more" and "few" leaves space for *some* truth claims. Ultimately McFague does want to affirm that we can speak of the divine—not *in se* but *pro nobis*—and that some metaphors correspond to the divine reality more faithfully than others. In this she stands closer to Christ.

McFague defends the truthfulness of her proposals on pragmatic grounds. How do we determine if a metaphor or model—a model is a constellation of metaphors with "staying power"[11]—is appropriate? McFague's response is essentially pragmatic. Metaphors and models are not descriptive; there is no way to say one is "truer" than another in any absolute referential sense. Rather, metaphors and models are prescriptive. They shape a way of being in the world. As McFague says, "A theologian's job is to help Christians think about God, other people—and nature—so that we *can, will, act differently toward them*."[12] Thus there is a pragmatic ethical norm for metaphors and models. McFague sees it as her role as a Christian theologian to deconstruct and reconstruct Christian symbols such that they foster liberating praxis.[13]

Yet this is not the whole story. McFague also grounds her metaphorical ventures in core beliefs that she holds. Two critical ones from her early work include the reality of God and the *imago Dei*. Regarding the reality of God, she writes: "Christian faith is . . . most basically a claim that the universe is neither indifferent nor malevolent but that there is a power (and a personal power at that) which is on the side of life and its fulfillment."[14] In this early form this may appear to be a statement only of the normative

---

9. McFague, *Models of God*, 60–61.
10. Reynolds, "Two McFagues," 295.
11. McFague, *Models of God*, 34.
12. McFague, *Super, Natural Christians*, 67 (my emphasis).
13. McFague, *Body of God*, 67–68.
14. McFague, *Models of God*, x.

role of God-language in the Christian cultural-linguistic paradigm; indeed it may be just that for McFague at this point. But her later work makes clear (as we will see) that the existence of a loving divine reality is a "background belief" for her. She does not reason to it; she reasons from it. The reality of a divine referent prevents theological discourse from sliding into nihilism and relativism.

McFague also affirms the centrality of *imago Dei*:

> I have emphasized the word "person" for two reasons. First, we are created in the image of God (Genesis 3:27), so we now, with the model of Jesus, have further support for imagining God in our image, the image of persons. This means that personal, relational images are central in a metaphorical theology—images of God as father, mother, lover, friend, savior, ruler, governor, servant, companion, comrade, liberator, and so on . . . . This need not be seen as crude anthropomorphism, but as foundational language, the dominant model, of God-talk.[15]

This is a crucial affirmation for McFague because it permits her language to make (perhaps soft) ontological truth claims. Theological language is not merely pragmatic and instrumental. It is grounded in the divine reality and it can make normative claims because the *imago Dei* permits true (if indirect) speech about God and the world.

In her later work McFague picks up the language of the "relative absolute": a "deeply held abiding insight into God's relation to us."[16] The relative absolute is the "central encompassing insight" around which a theologian spins her or his theological vision. McFague even uses the language of revelation: "Revelation is an insight about God and the world that changes your life."[17] For McFague what has been revealed, her "relative absolute," is this: "We live to give God glory by loving the world and everything in it."[18] This emphasis on the relative absolute coincides with Christ's insistence that theological language, while subject to vicissitudes of context, may nevertheless be intended to refer to divine reality because it is grounded in and the result of "embodied thinking": commitments "shaped by . . . felt experience, tempered by reflection."[19]

15. McFague, *Metaphorical Theology*, 27.
16. McFague, *Life Abundant*, 29.
17. Ibid., 54.
18. Ibid., 10.
19. Quoted in Reynolds, "Two McFagues," 294.

Of course McFague is quick to point to the "relative, all-too-human" nature of the "relative absolute," and this necessitates the metaphorical character of theological discourse.[20] One thing we can say definitively is this: for McFague, religious language—indeed, all language—is necessarily metaphorical.[21] She takes an essentially Kantian perspective: we cannot know things-in-themselves, only things-as-they-appear-to-us. Because we cannot know things-in-themselves, we use metaphors as a way of pointing to what ultimately cannot be named, "carrying over" (*meta-phor*) meaning from the known to the unknown (and presumably vice versa: metaphors for the unknown reshape our understanding of the known). As McFague describes it: "Most simply, a metaphor is seeing one thing as something else, pretending 'this' is 'that' because we do not know how to think or talk about 'this,' so we use 'that' as a way of saying something about it."[22] Of course this is not new; thinkers in the Christian theological tradition have generally recognized that God eludes our language and concepts and so all our attempts to speak and think about God are partial and incomplete. Because of this incapacity of language to "grasp" God, McFague argues we have tremendous (though not quite unlimited) freedom to experiment with metaphors.

It is important to note both the "is" and an "is-not" quality of metaphors for McFague.[23] They both carry over meaning ("is") but also negate meaning ("is-not"). To say that God is "mother," for example, is both to affirm that some meaning from the human experience of motherhood can rightly be carried over to God (say, that God is life-giving source, etc.) and also to deny that God is "really" a mother (God is not biologically female, etc.). Ellen Armour describes this "is/is-not" character of McFague's metaphorical approach as a balancing of traditionally Catholic sacramentalism ("is") with traditionally Protestant iconoclasm ("is-not").[24] This balancing of sacramentalism with iconoclasm affirms both the power of our metaphors to signify (though there is some ambiguity in McFague on this point), while also necessitating a plurality of metaphors because none is a true "fit." This plurality, in turn, helps to avoid literalism and to destabilize theological hierarchies, thus mitigating the formation of domination sys-

---

20. McFague, *Life Abundant*, 29.
21. McFague, *Metaphorical Theology*, 16.
22. Ibid., 15.
23. McFague, *Models of God*, 33.
24. Armour, "Toward an Elemental Theology," 47.

tems. The metaphor of God as "father," for example, has traditionally been reified (idolized), giving rise to a hierarchal structure that places males (and a particular vision of the male self) at the top. McFague's approach seeks to destabilize any such reified image with new (and sometimes unsettling) metaphors that undermine potentially oppressive hierarchies and engender liberative praxis.

We may rightly ask, from where does McFague's norm of liberative praxis come? She looks to Scripture, tradition, and experience as sources and resources for her vision. The experience of liberation (or the experience of God's transforming love) is primary. However:

> To claim that experience is the primary category is not . . . to say that religious experience is the basic criterion for a Christian theology or that we experience apart from or outside formative, linguistic communities: it is only to say that all our texts, including Scripture and the classics of the theological tradition, are "sedimentations" of interpreted experience.[25]

In this McFague is affirming both an experiential-expressivist and a cultural-linguistic approach (to borrow George Lindbeck's terms from *The Nature of Doctrine*). Experience may be the primary category, but all experience is radically embedded in culture and language. Likewise, cultural-linguistic formation makes possible certain otherwise inaccessible kinds of experience. Arguably McFague's whole methodology depends on this point: changing the metaphors we use to construe God and the world changes our experience of and praxis toward God and the world.

The experience of liberation, as this has been interpreted in and through the classics of the Christian theological tradition, is of central importance. This experience is always embedded in culture and language, to be sure, but McFague is willing to wager, following the tradition, that these experiences of liberation are clues to the reality of God. And if God is on the side of liberation, then liberation becomes a (perhaps *the*) key norm for theology.

Another important source and norm for McFague's theological method is what she calls postmodern science. By postmodern science, McFague appears to mean science that has been stripped of reductionism, mechanism, atomism, and so forth. (She does not give a straightforward definition of postmodern science, so we have to infer.) She rejects "scientism" (not her word), that is, science that fails to recognize its constructed nature

25. McFague, *Models of God*, 42.

and its appropriate limits. Postmodern science, however, is very important for McFague. She repeatedly argues that theologians must take seriously the view of reality current in their day, and in our day this view is shaped primarily by science. Theologians need not allow science to control their constructive work, but their work should be coherent within and compatible with the broad picture of (scientific) reality.

We see this most clearly in the use McFague makes of the "common creation story"—that is, the cosmological narrative of how everything came into being through a 13.7 billion year process of creative evolution, beginning with a tiny singularity and evolving to and through human self-consciousness. McFague finds great significance in this story, seeing it as affirming our common origin and destiny, our unity (we are all "star stuff") and our almost infinite diversity (the bewildering fecundity of the creative process). She also sees ethical implications in the common creation story:

> The common creation story is more than a scientific affair; it is, implicitly, deeply moral, for it raises the question of the place of human beings in nature, and calls for a kind of praxis in which we see ourselves in proportion, in harmony, and in a fitting manner relating to all others that live and all the systems that support life.[26]

The common creation story serves both to *decenter* humans—we are part of rather than lords over nature (*contra* Descartes)—and to *re-center* humans—so far as we know, we are the only forms of life in the universe capable of self-consciousness. We are the only creatures who know that we know. Thus we are the only creatures who know the common creation story and can shape our praxis accordingly.

Thus McFague's methodology ties together a number of disparate strands, some of which remain in a (hopefully creative) tension: historicism and suspicion of correspondence theories of truth and strong ontological claims; "embodied thinking" that recognizes the appropriateness of tying (weak) ontological claims to lived experience, to the "relative absolute" that fuels our thinking; the metaphoricity of all language, theological and otherwise; the importance of credibility vis-à-vis our "postmodern scientific" world view; and the centrality of liberating praxis as the pragmatic criterion for theological truth and the grounding of that criterion in the Christian story. She states her justification in simple terms: "I believe it. I believe it is Christian. I believe it is good for the world."[27] "I believe it"—it is

---

26. McFague, *Body of God*, 111.
27. Ibid., 29.

grounded in the revealed "relative absolute"; "I believe it is Christian"—it is consonant with the Christian classics of Scripture and tradition; "I believe it is good for the world"—it is both consonant with what we know about the world through other modes of discourse (science) and it fosters the liberative praxis the world so desperately needs. Or again: "All we can say is that from our own experience and within the parameters of our tradition, we have been persuaded to stand on this or that carefully thought-through interpretation of God's relation to the world."[28]

To sum up: McFague's methodology is shaped by liberative praxis. Both experience and tradition (which is the "sedimentation" of experience), while embedded in cultural-linguistic context, link experiences of liberation with the power and presence of God. Words about God (theology) should foster liberating praxis. Given the inherently metaphorical nature of all language, we are free to deploy a plurality of metaphors and models in our imaging of God and the world. Of course these metaphors and models must be credible; they must be compatible with the overall (scientific) picture of reality current in our day. But the ultimate test of these metaphors and models will be pragmatic and ethical: if we "try them on," if we live them out, do they empower liberative praxis?

Divine (Dis-)Embodiment: The Model of the World as God's Body

Perhaps McFague's best known metaphorical venture toward liberative praxis is the model of the world as God's body. What difference might it make, she wonders, "to think and act as if bodies matter"?[29] Her focus on embodiment is motivated significantly by her analysis of the ecological crisis. Among the many causes of distorted and destructive human attitudes toward nature are dualistic and spiritualizing tendencies that sacrifice the good of concrete bodies in the name of "higher" spiritual goods.[30] But McFague recognizes that bodies are a central category for all forms of oppression, whether the domination of the earth, or women, or other oppressed peoples. The valorization of male/spirit/culture over against female/body/nature has a long, seemingly universal, and profoundly de-

---

28. McFague, *Life Abundant*, 29.

29. Ibid., viii.

30. This is one of Lynn White's many critiques of the Christian attitude toward nature in his famous/infamous 1967 essay, "The Historical Roots of Our Ecologic Crisis."

structive history.[31] Thus a revalorization of bodies could serve not only an ecological agenda, but other liberating agendas as well. The fundamental truth is: everything that exists has a body (at least in the broad sense that McFague is using the term). Bodies go all the way up and all the way down; to be is to be embodied. And so bodies are at once the most intimate (we *are* our bodies), the most universal (everything is embodied), and potentially the most liberating way to think about reality.

McFague juxtaposes her organic model with what she calls the "classic" organic model, seen (according to her read of intellectual history) in the Greek stoics and in Origen and distorted somewhat by Augustine and Aquinas. While the "classic" organic model tended to value the spiritual over the bodily, thus rendering nature, bodies, women, and sexuality problematic, McFague's organic model begins and ends with bodies and eschews dualisms (at least in intent, if not in effect, as we will see). Additionally, while the "classic" organic model imagined one male heterosexual body (the Body of Christ), thus authorizing male hierarchy and denigrating difference, McFague's organic model emphasizes a multiplicity of bodies and rejects anthropocentrism and androcentrism.[32] The organic model is for McFague a crucial component of a paradigm shift:

> [F]rom heaven to earth; from otherworldly to this worldly; from above to below; from a distant, external God to a near, immanental God; from time and history to space and land; from soul to body; from individualism to community; from mechanistic to organic thinking; from spiritual salvation to holistic well-being; from anthropocentrism to cosmocentrism.[33]

McFague invites us into a thought (and ultimately life) experiment: to imagine all the matter of the universe, all the bodies of the universe taken together, as comprising a single body: the body of God.[34]

She offers three warrants for such a model. First, it illuminates the paradigmatic story of Jesus:

---

31. See for example Ruether, *Sexism and God-Talk*, chapter 3, and Ortner's essay "Is Female to Male as Nature Is to Culture?"

32. McFague, *Body of God*, 30–38.

33. McFague, *Life Abundant*, 131.

34. This raises an important question: if all the bodies of the universe together make up the "body of God," to what extent can we call this a body at all, even analogically? Is not a body defined in part by its limits, its boundaries, by the way it stands over against other bodies? What "body" does the universe stand over against?

> How should we understand the presence of God to the world . . . ? In some way, the surprising invitation to the oppressed, to the last and the least, expressed in the parables, the table fellowship, and the cross needs to be imaginatively perceived as permanently present in every present and every space: it needs to be grasped, in the most profound sense, as a worldly reality . . . . [W]hat if we were to understand the resurrection and ascension not as the bodily translation of some individuals to another world—a mythology no longer credible to us—but as the promise of God to be permanently present, "bodily" present to us, in all places and times of our world?[35]

In other words, the model of the world as God's body gives us a credible way of talking and thinking about the presence of God in the world to which the paradigmatic story of Jesus points.

A second warrant for the model of the world as God's body is that it is congruous with the common creation story. Science images the universe, not as a machine, but as an organism, interconnected and interdependent, encompassing unity and difference. This invites organic/bodily metaphors.

The third and primary warrant for the model of the world as God's body is ethical. This becomes especially clear when McFague juxtaposes the organic/world-as-God's-body model with the monarchial/God-as-sovereign model. McFague sees much that is destructive in the monarchial model: God is imaged as transcendent to and distant from the world (at least as McFague construes transcendence); God has to do primarily or exclusively with human beings; God is sovereign and not impinged upon by the world, thus setting up both a potentially oppressive hierarchy and a model of "self-sufficiency" to be imitated by (primarily) males, with disastrous results[36]; and ultimately what is real and has value is what transcends the world and matter and bodies, thus inscribing a hierarchy of spirit over body that carries with it hierarchies of male over female and human over nature, among other structures of subjugation.

McFague's organic model is intended as a corrective to all of this. God is imaged as intimately related to the world (indeed, as intimately related to the world as we are to our bodies); God is related to all creation, not just humans, thus eschewing anthropocentrism (which typically manifests as androcentrism as well); God is imaged not as a supremely "separative

---

35. McFague, *Models of God*, 60.
36. See for example Keller, *From a Broken Web*, 33–38.

self" but as vulnerable to the world[37]; and the model valorizes bodies overagainst spirit/body hierarchies. Thus McFague believes the organic model, the model of the world as God's body, generates better ethics, a more liberative praxis, than the monarchial model.

It is hard to imagine a stronger affirmation of the immanence of God than the model of the world as God's body. Some might argue that God is so immanent in this model that it risks collapsing into pantheism. In response to this, and in an effort to maintain continuity with the Christian tradition, McFague introduces a second model intended to affirm the transcendent agency of God. God is not pure immanence in/as the world. God is also transcendent agent, active within but not identical with the world. So McFague speaks of God as the life-giving spirit and breath that flows to and through all creation, the spirit that enlivens the body.[38]

She speaks of five models of the God-world relation. Three—deism, dialogical, and monarchial—are ruled out as potentially if not necessarily destructive. The two remaining models—agential and organic—are each inadequate without the other. McFague intends to bring these two together, agential and organic, transcendent and immanent, breath-of-God and body-of-God, in a panentheistic dialectic. She says: "We are suggesting that we think of God metaphorically as the spirit that is the breath, the life of the universe, a universe that comes from God and could be seen as the body of God."[39]

There is a third dimension to this model (or these models) for McFague. Christians will want to lay a "superimposition" on to this model of the world as God's body: the body of Christ. That is, Christians will give "Christic" shape to God's body.[40] This is critically important, because drawing an ethic from the common creation story, besides potentially running afoul of the naturalistic fallacy, also runs afoul of natural selection. That is, one of the things we learn from the common creation story (which McFague at times seems to play down) is that the mechanism of natural

---

37. "Separative self" comes from Keller (see above). Later we will consider the extent to which God is truly vulnerable to the world in McFague's model.

38. McFague, *Body of God*, 141–50.

39. Ibid., 144. This quote may be most noteworthy for its hedging. It points to the challenge of holding these two models together.

40. This raises the question: what was the shape of God's body *before* this Christic superimposition?

selection rewards the fit and disposes of the unfit. The Christic paradigm comes as a direct counter to that.[41]

The distinctive Christian contribution is precisely the shape Jesus' parables, healings, and eating practices give to the world as God's body. As McFague describes it, the Christic paradigm has a *deconstructive* phase, seen in Jesus' parables, which undermine and overturn oppressive hierarchies; a *reconstructive* phase, seen in Jesus' healing stories, which promote physical sustainability and bodily thriving; and a *prospective* phase, seen in Jesus' eating practices, which point toward the future inclusion of everyone at the table.[42] Each of these phases is inclusive of nature as well as humanity. McFague acknowledges that "it is futile to rummage about with fig trees and hens, trying to make Jesus into a nature lover."[43] Nevertheless, in his parables, healings, and eating practices Jesus models an alternative vision of the relationship between humans and nature. Evolution may select for the fit, but the world as God's body superimposed with the cosmic Christ selects for the unfit, the weak, and the poor (including nature as "the new poor"[44]), liberating and healing and including all.

McFague has now invited us to hold three models together: the world as God's body, God as spirit and breath of life, and God as seen in and through the Christic paradigm. Perhaps not surprisingly, she turns to the doctrine of the Trinity as a way of holding these three in creative tension. McFague argues that the purpose of the doctrine of the Trinity is precisely to preserve both the immanence and the transcendence of God, which is what her composite model is attempting to do. So we have the mystery of God, the invisible face of God, the first person of the Trinity; we have the physicality of God, the visible body of God, the second person of the Trinity; and we have the mediation of the invisible to the visible, the mediating spirit, the third person of the Trinity.[45] Through McFague's construal of the Trinity, we affirm God as mystery, "the one before whom words recoil" as Shankara says; God as embodied in and as the world, though for Christians this embodiment is seen in and through the Christic paradigm; and God as

---

41. See Theissen, *Biblical Faith*, for an interesting discussion of the Jesus movement as a counter-evolutionary mutation in human consciousness.
42. McFague, *Body of God*, 188–89.
43. McFague, *Life Abundant*, 167.
44. Ibid., xii.
45. Ibid., 193.

the life-giving spirit and breath that mediates between the mystery and the body, the invisible and the visible.

There is much that is promising in McFague's model, perhaps most centrally the revalorizing of bodies. This is crucial because, as we have already noted, bodies are the "common denominator" in many forms of oppression. In one sense this is obvious: we *are* bodies, so how else can we be oppressed but in and through our bodies? But there is a deeper issue. Any time a dualism is permitted between body and spirit/mind, a dangerous hierarchy potentially is established, one that allows male (spirit/mind) to dominate female (body), or humans to dominate nature (which is construed as female and bodily), or white people to dominate people of color (who are construed as more bodily), or Christians to dominate non-Christians (saving their souls while sacrificing their bodies), and so on. If God is embodied, then perhaps we can look to our own bodies and the bodies of others not as sources of shame or defilement, nor as something to escape or something to be subdued by "higher" faculties, but as sacred and worthy of reverence and care. Reverence for the body has the potential to overturn systems of domination: you cannot reverence a person's body and simultaneously destroy it. Expand this to nature as God's body, and a potentially robust environmental ethic begins to take shape.

There are other promising aspects of McFague's model that we do not have space to explore but that deserve brief mention: the destabilizing, antihierarchical quality of her methodology; her strong emphasis on liberating praxis as the norm for theological construction; her embrace of (postmodern) science and the common creation story (though this brings with it many challenges, as we will see); her emphasis on the interconnectedness and interdependence of all things; her efforts to resist anthropocentrism and androcentrism and with it a purely utilitarian view of nature, while at the same time affirming the unique capacities and responsibilities human beings have as the (apparently) only self-conscious participants in the evolutionary process; her extension of the meaning-field of Jesus' parables, healing stories, and eating practices to include nature—all of these are significant contributions to an ecological theology that fosters liberative praxis toward nature.

However, there are significant challenges with McFague's model. I will note three. First, while I appreciate the way her methodology encourages playfulness and creativity and risk-taking, at times "metaphoricity" seems to be a way of evading difficult questions. A model as radical as the world as God's body raises important questions; many of those questions seem to be declared out of bounds with the reminder that this is "only" a metaphor. Michael S. Northcott critiques McFague on this point: "Environmental philosophers do not resort to this linguistic sleight of hand [dismissing questions by claiming all religious language is analogical]. Why should ecotheologians?"[46] Put another way, while I appreciate the value of McFague's metaphorical approach, it raises a number of metaphysical questions that her method does not permit her to address.

An example of this is McFague's discussion of the God-world relation. She deploys metaphors that are intended to express God's relation to the world (agential/spirit metaphors and organic/body metaphors), but she has no way conceptually of talking about this relation. This is especially problematic because her commitment to science leaves very few cracks for God to "sneak through." She insists that theologians must take seriously the (scientific) picture of the world; she also insists models and metaphors must be credible. But she gives us no credible way of talking about the God-world relation within the context of science. As Byron Bangert puts it:

> McFague's notion of divine agency seems to amount to little more than vitalism. God provides no direction or purpose *until* the emergence of self-consciousness, at which point evolution is not only biological but also historical and cultural.[47]

With no credible way to speak of God's action in the world, it is difficult to maintain that McFague has been successful in preserving the agential aspects of the Christian conception of God.

McFague's embrace of science poses a second challenge. Lisa Sideris critiques McFague for not taking seriously enough the implications of Darwinian evolution and natural selection. McFague's ecological model, says Sideris, is

> closer to the Romantic ecology of the eighteenth and early nineteenth centuries (as well as ecosystem concepts of fifty years ago) than it is to a cutting-edge, postmodern scientific perspective she professes to adopt.[48]

---

46. Northcott, *Environment and Christian Ethics*, 160.

47. Bangert, *Consenting to God and Nature*, 138.

48. Sideris, *Environmental Ethics*, 70.

It is unfair to suggest that McFague is unaware of the difficulties natural selection poses. She is quite explicit that the Christic paradigm is a form of resistance to natural selection.[49] Christians living in and through the Christic paradigm are attempting to "bend evolution" toward a more liberating, healing, inclusive trajectory.

Nevertheless, Sideris may be justified in critiquing the implicit individualism and the eschatological dimensions of McFague's ethic. As Sideris says: "McFague's ethic falsely imagines that nature functions in a way that permits the flourishing of every individual creature at once."[50] The thriving of each individual may be consistent with certain construals of Christianity, but it is not consistent with the natural selection process. Likewise with Sideris' critique of McFague's eschatology: "It is simply the peaceable kingdom, *a corrective to nature as it really is*."[51] This is significant because McFague has argued that human beings should approach nature with a "loving eye"—an eye which respects the alterity of the other—rather than with an "arrogant eye" which bends everything to its subjectivity.[52] Is an eschatological vision of the lion and the lamb feeding together, nature "purified" of predation and natural selection—is this vision seen with the "loving eye" or the "arrogant eye"? We will have more to say about McFague's eschatology in a moment.

A third, and perhaps the greatest, challenge to McFague's model is its inherent instability. To put it simply, she asks the model to do too much. She recognizes this: her organic model cannot preserve both the immanence and the transcendence of God, both the embodied and the agential aspects of God. So she adds another model: God as spirit and breath of life. But this cannot deliver the ethical norms she desires, so she adds a third model: the superimposition of the Christic paradigm onto the model of the world as God's body. It feels a bit like ancient astronomers trying to prop up the geocentric model by adding epicycles to make the model fit the data. Eventually the whole thing becomes cumbersome and incoherent. McFague's brief trinitarian reflections do not, in my judgment, relieve the strain.

This instability results in large part from the "broken" nature of her root metaphor. McFague intends for us to draw an analogy between human

---

49. McFague, *Body of God*, 173.
50. Sideris, *Environmental Ethics*, 82.
51. Ibid., 83 (my emphasis).
52. See McFague, *Body of God*, chapter 2.

embodiment and God's embodiment.⁵³ As she says, the "universe is a body, to use a poor analogy from our own experience, but it is not a human body; rather it is matter bodied forth seemingly infinitely, diversely, endlessly, yet internally as one."⁵⁴ But this raises a whole nexus of questions around the concept of bodies and embodiment. From a scientific perspective, which McFague espouses, we are not embodied so much as we *are bodies*. We are not *in* our bodies; we *are* our bodies. Mind and consciousness are emergent properties. They emerge from the brain and are dependent upon the brain. Clearly McFague does not want to say this about God. "Everything that is is *in* God and God is *in* all things and yet God is not identical with the universe, *for the universe is dependent on God in a way that God is not dependent on the universe*."⁵⁵ God cannot be imagined as an emergent property of the universe; this would be out of bounds for Christian theological discourse. So in what sense can we speak of God as being embodied? *What is embodied?*

It seems that in her efforts to preserve divine transcendence, McFague is smuggling dualism back into the picture. God may be embodied spirit, but ultimately God is not dependent on the world/body. Does this not suggest that God is *really* spirit and only secondarily embodied, and that spirit is higher because it is not dependent on the body? If we take these implications and shift the metaphor back toward human beings, we pick up (or simply reinscribe) that same dualism of mind/spirit over body, along with all the destructive implications in terms of hierarchies and oppressive structures. McFague recognizes this danger, and in her earlier work she says: "to model ourselves after this God [a God who is not dependent on the world/body] is to want to escape from the confines of the body."⁵⁶ However, she may not be successful in heeding her own warning.

Mark Wallace critiques McFague along these lines, suggesting that ultimately she pulls back from a "no-holds-barred" incarnationalism, rendering her model unstable.

> If the world is God's body, and if "being embodied" (as opposed to simply "having a body") entails that an entity is fundamentally

---

53. See ibid., 139, 145, 194.
54. Ibid., 96–97.
55. Ibid., 149 (my emphasis).
56. McFague, *Models of God*, 112.

dependent on its body for its well-being, then in what sense is God both bodily and yet not dependent on God's body?[57]

It seems that McFague wants to have it both ways: to affirm both God's identity with and independence from the universe. As Wallace notes, God is only seemingly "at risk" in creation. In reality God is safely other than the universe.

Perhaps there are ways to preserve the model of the world as God's body without reinscribing a destructive dualism. Wallace encourages a full-turn to incarnationalism, with the implication that ecocide risks deicide.[58] This is reminiscent of Hans Jonas's post-Holocaust concept of God, a radically "at-risk" God whose "face" is beatified or distorted irrevocably by the unpredictable unfolding of creation.[59] There are perhaps resonances here with process thought (for which McFague expresses some appreciation), where God's consequent nature is determined by God's experience with the world (though, *contra* Wallace and Jonas, God's primordial nature is still "safely" other). Whatever we are to make of such possibilities, they are at least consistent workings out of the implications of a strong emphasis on immanence in the God-world relation.

If McFague is disinclined to move in these directions, and all the evidence suggests that she is, perhaps a reemphasis on the transcendence and otherness of God, combined with her affirmation of the interconnectedness and interdependence of all things (drawn from the common creation story), all circumscribed within a stronger eschatological perspective, might be fruitful. Arguably we see something like this in Teilhard de Chardin. In this perspective, to paraphrase Deuteronomy, all nature is "a wandering Aramean." It is not human beings alone wandering through an empty landscape in search of a heavenly kingdom. It is rather all creation (humans included) wandering through space and time, drawn by God toward sabbath rest (with echoes of Moltmann, to be sure). Granted at this point we have moved well beyond the metaphorical field of bodies, but such a perspective may still have the potential to generate the kind of liberative praxis McFague so strongly advocates. Of course such a move invites a deeper consideration of McFague's explicit and implicit eschatology.

---

57. Wallace, *Fragments of the Spirit*, 140.
58. Ibid., 141.
59. Jonas, "The Concept of God after Auschwitz."

"Only If": McFague's Subjunctive Eschatology

Describing McFague's eschatology is challenging, for several reasons. Eschatology is not frequently considered explicitly in her work. One finds threads of discussion here or there and must stitch them together to try to create a more coherent picture. Unlike Moltmann, for whom eschatology is "the medium of Christian faith as such, the key in which everything in it is set, the glow that suffuses everything here in the dawn of an unexpected new day,"[60] for McFague eschatology is not a central consideration. She rarely explicitly critiques the Christian eschatological tradition, but it is safe to assume she is concerned about its absolutizing and totalizing potentiality, echoing her critique of "classical theism" more generally. A further complication is that, as with so much in McFague's theology, her eschatological perspective shifts and evolves. This is due both to her methodological commitment to plurality and playfulness, and also to what I interpret to be a significant shift in her (for lack of a better expression) "existential engagement" with her theological work, marked explicitly in *Life Abundant*. Here I will try to draw together some of the various threads of eschatological reflection we find in McFague.

In *Models of God* McFague's use of eschatological language reflects what Moltmann would call a "presentative" orientation: the resurrection is "the promise of God to be permanently present, 'bodily' present to us, in all places and times of our world."[61] In other words, the resurrection signals God's irrevocable commitment to embodiment (though precisely how irrevocable that commitment is for McFague is a matter of contention, as previously noted). McFague's language of "promise" obscures what my language of "signal" makes more explicit: that the resurrection is a revealing of what is always and everywhere already the case. It is not the promise of the coming of something new (Moltmann's *novum*); it is the promise of the continuation of what has always ever been: God's embodied presence.

In *The Body of God*, however, McFague's eschatological language takes on a greater future orientation. She suggests that what is "hinted at" in the resurrection is "that bodies, all suffering bodies, will live again to see a new day."[62] Here a future orientation becomes central, though McFague immediately shrouds it in qualifications, confessing that it is difficult to imagine

---

60. Moltmann, "My Theological Career," 170.
61. McFague, *Models of God*, 60.
62. McFague, *Body of God*, 174.

resurrection, then or now. However, a few pages later she gives a more full-throated affirmation of a future-oriented eschatology:

> We must believe in the basic trustworthiness at the heart of existence; that life, not death, is the last word; that against all evidence to the contrary (and most evidence is to the contrary), all our efforts on behalf of the well-being of our planet and especially of its most vulnerable creatures, including the human ones, will not be defeated.[63]

This striking affirmation suggests that the God seen in the resurrection will bring all things to "well-being"—or at least, that we must believe that it is so. (Presumably we must believe this in order to foster ethical action.) It is not altogether clear what kind of future McFague is committing herself to here. Given the way she grants normative status to science, does her Moltmann-like affirmation that the "well-being" of "vulnerable creatures, including human ones, will not be defeated" commit her to a future that stands in contrast to any conceivable scientific future? That is, would the extinction of the human creature (as is seemingly all but inevitable) stand as evidence against McFague's eschatology, as a failure of the God of resurrection to prevent death from getting the last word? Is McFague's reliance on science and the common creation story an eschatological liability, given science's dim view of the world's future?

However, this is not the final resting place for McFague's eschatology. When she turns to eschatology explicitly in *The Body of God*, we hear a different voice. Here she speaks of the future as "goad and goal," and the future not as utopia but as atopia, "an imagined world both prophetic and alluring from which we can judge what is wrong" with our present reality.[64] She describes several "notes of a new creation." Central to this eschatological articulation is *vision* (similar to Teilhard in the previous chapter), seeing things in the proper light. First is the realization of interdependence and independence. Awareness of this interdependent and independent existence leads to an appropriate way of being situated within complex ecosystemic realities, a way of being that both acknowledges webs of interconnectedness but also values the individual. Second is the affirmation that salvation in this emerging eschatological paradigm is focused "first of all" on the physical needs of the earth's creatures. (It is not clear that McFague ever moves beyond this "first of all", at least in this discussion.) Of course salvation in

63. Ibid., 191.
64. Ibid., 198.

this sense must be extended to all embodied creatures, and so we are called to solidarity with all those who are oppressed. Finally McFague emphasizes the vocation of human creatures in this vision: as the only creatures seemingly possessed of self-awareness, we have a unique obligation to be the stewards of life in creation.[65]

I am certainly sympathetic with McFague's call to action and responsibility here. And in some ways there is nothing surprising in this; it is simply another statement of her overarching argument in *The Body of God*. What *is* surprising is that this entire discussion takes place under the rubric of eschatology. McFague's "notes of a new creation" are a call to see creation as it always already is—interconnected and interdependent—and to respond ethically to that reality (by bringing salvation to broken bodies). And while McFague certainly wishes to affirm that God empowers the whole process, ultimately the eschatological future rests in the hands of human beings with their special vocation.

This tension—McFague wishing to affirm a hopeful eschatology (what we "must" believe) while ultimately restricting eschatological hope to what human beings (empowered by God, to be sure) can accomplish ("if only" human beings act) becomes even more pronounced in her later work. I indicated before that *Life Abundant* represents a shift in McFague's "existential engagement" with her work. McFague states this explicitly. In her religious autobiography she names four conversions in her life: first, in her youth, a burgeoning awareness both of the possibility of nonbeing and a concomitant wonder at being, and attaching the word "God" to the source of wonderful being; second, a Barthian phase of emphasizing transcendence standing in tension with her experience of God's immanent beauty in nature; third, the piercing of her consciousness (provoked by Gordon Kaufmann) of the reality of the nuclear and ecological crises and what they mean for theology; and fourth, what Bonhoeffer calls "becoming contemporary with God."[66]

It is this fourth conversion to which I have been alluding. For McFague it takes the form of a more robust affirmation of the loving reality of God (beneath and behind all our metaphorical ventures) and a spiritual practice that gradually shifts the center of her existence from self to God. This last conversion is significant for our purposes because it intensifies the hopeful side of McFague's eschatology; at times her eschatological language in *Life*

---

65. Ibid., 198–202.
66. McFague, *Life Abundant*, 8.

Abundant can sound very much like Moltmann. And yet even here there is a crucial limiting factor.

There are lines of continuity, of course, between her eschatological affirmations in *Life Abundant* and previous affirmations. She speaks of Jesus' resurrection as the "hope that the love of God for the dispossessed and oppressed will not die but live again for us and in us."[67] This is consistent with McFague's earlier claims in that it seems to deny (or to be indifferent toward) the event character of the resurrection (it is a "hope," not an event) and also—and this will become more important going forward—in the intimation that resurrection hope is somehow tied to human vocation: that is, the hope that it will live "in us." Later she echoes her words from *The Body of God*:

> "God" is the belief that hope and not despair, life not death, laughter not tears are deep in the nature of things and that while despair, death, and tears are necessary part of reality they are not the dominant part.[68]

Despite the curiously non-realist language ("God" is a "belief") this is consistent with her earlier affirmations that eschatological hope is tied not so much to a future possibility as to a present reality. This is how things *are*; our hope comes from seeing them as such.

But despite these lines of continuity, McFague's eschatology is stretched even further in *Life Abundant*. In what may be the most helpful summary of her whole project, she writes of what we need from an ecological Christology:

> the appreciation of the intrinsic worth of all life-forms, not just of human beings; the need to turn to earth, respecting it and caring for it in local, ordinary, mundane ways; the acknowledgement that human salvation or well-being and nature's health are intrinsically connected; the insistence on justice to the oppressed, including nature, and the realization that solidarity with the oppressed will result in cruciform living for the affluent; the recognition that God is with us, embodied not only in Jesus of Nazareth but in all of nature, thus uniting creation and sanctifying bodily life; *and, finally, a promise of a renewed creation through the hope of resurrection, a*

---

67. McFague, *Life Abundant*, 20.
68. Ibid., 155.

promise that includes the entire cosmos and speaks to our ecological despair.[69]

McFague ties together resurrection and hope for a new creation. She writes approvingly of an eschatological Christology, even quoting Moltmann:

> Eschatological christologies such as those of Moltmann and Keller underscore renewal and hope: God's Spirit working in Christ recreates, transforms, the entire universe toward reconciliation and peace. As the firstborn of the new creation the resurrected Christ symbolizes the power of life over death. Nothing, no scrap of creation, will be excluded from this new life: "the body of Christ is the whole cosmos."[70]

Here, especially with Moltmann's reference to the whole cosmos as the body of Christ, McFague and Moltmann seem very close to each other. Echoing Moltmann's comments on "universal Easter laughter," McFague rejects the claim that Christianity is finally a tragic vision. The resurrection "symbolizes" (her word) the triumph of life over death, and that the God who is on the side of life and fulfillment and is also on our side.[71]

However, it seems clear that for McFague the resurrection represents the *possibility* of life conquering death, not the reality: subjunctive, not indicative. And thus the presence of the God of life with us and for us does not make a new reality; rather it empowers a new possibility. But that possibility is ultimately and finally contingent upon the human response.

McFague turns to the prophet Ezekiel and the "valley of dry bones" in chapter 37 to speak of the partnership between human creatures and God. God may have been the ultimate source of resurrection power, and of course God underlies and empowers the whole scene. Nevertheless, what is significant for McFague is that while God calls Ezekiel to speak, it is Ezekiel who must actually do the speaking. It is Ezekiel who prophesizes to the bones and calls the winds. McFague draws the lesson from this that the renewal of creation is ultimately a partnership between God (the source of life), the human creature (who must be a steward of life), and the wind (creation itself). As she transposes this scene from the Old Testament to our moment, she writes:

---

69. McFague, *Body of God* (italics mine).
70. Ibid., 164.
71. Ibid., 170.

> I see huge mounds of elephant bones, remnants of the ivory trade, the spindly remains of an old-growth forest after a clear-cut, and the visible skeleton of a starving child. Can they also live? Those who trust in the God of creation and recreation, the God of the resurrection, answer Yes—even these dry bones can live. *But, remembering the cruciform reality of Christian life, we must add, only if we, as partners of God, turn from ecological selfishness and life a different abundant life.*[72]

Once again I wish to affirm my sympathy for McFague's passion and vision. However, for the purposes of understanding her eschatology, her last sentence is most revealing. An "only if" hangs over her eschatological affirmation. God may be the God of creation and new creation; God may be the source of life; God may underlie and empower all creaturely reality. And yet, if these bones are to live again, it will happen *only if* human beings, the partners of God, live differently.

It is precisely here that the hopefulness of McFague's eschatology is stifled. God cannot (will not?) unilaterally bring about a new creation. The new creation can only come about through human striving. She repeats this pattern many times, linking a hopeful affirmation of new creation with concomitant conditional clauses:

> The resurrection is a promise from Reality Itself—from God—that life and love and joy and health and peace and beauty are stronger than their opposites—*if we help to make it so, if we will follow the way of Jesus, the way of cruciform living.*[73]

> The banquet of life was not just for her [speaking of Dorothy Day], but for everyone, and it was available now *if Christ's disciples would help it become so.*[74]

> God is able to bring this about [making every creature fully alive], *through our willingness and work.*[75]

Each affirmation of hope is tied to the conditional human response. On the one hand, this is part of what sustains the humble dimensions of McFague's eschatology: she does not envision a divine unmaking and remaking of

---

72. Ibid., 171.
73. Ibid., 179.
74. Ibid., 193.
75. Ibid., 202.

the world. Whatever hopeful future there is for the world is tied to divine creativity, to be sure, but it is channeled through and limited by human creatures. There will be no new Jerusalem descending from the heavens, and, by extension, there will be no vegetarian lions. What will be is limited to what human creatures, called and inspired by God, can accomplish.

But this conditional hope is also what finally prevents McFague's eschatology from being truly hopeful. Her affirmation of science over against any kind of divine supernatural fiat has already shrunk her horizons: the sun will burn out, all life on earth will end. This already strains her affirmations of death not getting the last word. But combined with her insistence that new creation, limited though it may be, comes about only in and through human creatures, the hopefulness of her vision thins to the point of transparency. Who can look at the present condition of the human project and truly hope for human transformation? Who can look at our political and economic systems and find cause for anything other than despair? If God must wait for us, then all creation will wait, and the seas will rise.

How does one articulate a hopeful vision that encompasses all things, without doing violence to their fragile particularities? How does one cherish the tragic beauty of all things without succumbing to despair in the midst of their perpetual perishing? How does one have love and hope in the midst of a warming world? As with Moltmann, Sallie McFague walks the fault line between a hopeful orientation toward the future and a humble cherishing of the good, green earth. But despite her sometimes passionate rhetoric, her hope is finally curtailed by the bondage of the human will. If indeed the divine creativity at work in the world is restrained by human consent, given the vulnerability and the tragic structure of the human condition, given the resulting idolatry and concupiscence, perhaps we will need a more vital understanding of the possibility of human redemption in order to make hope a possibility.

4

Taking Our Stand with the Dirt

Humility and the Cosmic Process

Given the ecological diminishment that we are daily witnessing and contributing to, how do we maintain an orientation toward the future that is both humble, staying close to the good, green earth, and also hopeful, open to the fresh flowing of divine grace? This has been my driving question throughout this project. In this and the following chapter, I use these two rubrics—humility and hope—to begin tracing the contours of a response.

By humility I do not mean simply the virtue of being mindful of one's fallibility, frailty, and limitations, though this is certainly a virtue in need of cultivation. Nor do I mean the common and destructive distortion of this virtue into self-deception or self-loathing. Humility as I am using the term has deeper roots than that. To be humble is to be of the *humus*, the soil, the dirt. As Holmes Rolston reminds us, "ground constitutes our humble beginnings, whether called primordial stardust, organically rich soil, microbial material, or simply slime."[1]

To be humble is to be lowly, close to the ground. It is to be ever mindful of one's nature as *adam* of the *adamah*, a person of the soil, a child of the dust, an earthling, a dirty groundling.[2] To be humble is to remain ever mindful of the ways our origin and our destiny are inextricably interwoven with the origin and destiny of dirt. "All go to one place; all are from the

---

1. Rolston, *Three Big Bangs*, 96.
2. See Brown, *Seven Pillars of Creation*, 81.

dust, and all turn to dust again" (Eccl 3:20). Just as the human story cannot begin apart from the dirt, so it cannot end apart from the dirt. In contrast to any eschatological vision that imagines the dissolution of the earth as a means of liberation for the human animal, there is no dirt-free future for the earthling.

Of course dirt is never simply dirt. While it is possible in an urban, technological society to be so far removed from dirt as to consider it a nuisance rather than a nexus for life, in truth, a single handful of dirt is a conglomeration of information and fecundity, the creation of cosmic processes and local transformations.

> There is in a typical handful of humus, which may have 10 billion organisms in it, a richness of structure, a volume of information (trillions of "bits"), resulting from evolutionary processes across a billion years of history, greatly advanced over anything in myriads of galaxies, or even, so far as we know, all of them.[3]

Stars and planets are formed from interstellar dust and gas; heavy elements like carbon and iron—the building blocks of the world around us—are the dusty expulsions of dying stars. It was not just Joni Mitchell who sang that we are stardust; science concurs. The dirty groundling is a creature of stardust and stories, and the very dirt beneath our feet, the dust that comprises our bodies, opens out into the entire cosmic process. For that reason, humility begins by looking down to the dirt, but it does not end there, because the dirt itself draws our gaze upward and outward. If humility means staying grounded, standing in solidarity with the dirt, then it also means standing in solidarity with the entire cosmic process with which it and we are inextricably interwoven.

In what follows I will be tracing out the theologically germane contours of this cosmic process with which we are inextricably interwoven, what might otherwise be considered an embryonic doctrine of creation. Here I prefer the phrase "cosmic process" to "creation" for two principal reasons. First, *cosmic* process keeps us mindful of the immensity of the process that is unfolding before us and behind us and through us and beneath our feet. "Creation" risks becoming a bit too cozy compared to the vast reaches of cosmic process. We no longer occupy the comparably human-scaled, three-tiered universe of our ancestors. Second, cosmic *process* is a reminder of the dynamic, unfolding nature of the cosmos, that it is in

---

3. Rolston, *Three Big Bangs*, 49.

flux, in movement, evolving. No doubt there are structures and orderings, but these are not the fixed "orders of creation" that have at times attached themselves to doctrines of creation, often with deleterious consequences.[4]

What can—what must—we say of this cosmic process into which dirt opens up? Perhaps in keeping with humility in the smaller sense, there is much that we cannot say, much that theologians are tempted to venture for which we have no warrants. Here as elsewhere in this project I am inclined to keep my reflections close to the ground, to the sources, dynamics, trajectories, and possibilities that can be discerned in the cosmic process itself and the way those sources, dynamics, trajectories, and possibilities can be interpreted through the lens of the Christian scriptural and theological tradition.

If humility is remaining grounded in the *humus*, and the *humus* opens out to the entire cosmic process, then humility is solidarity with and consent to precisely *this* cosmic process, and not some other. I intend the following tracings to flesh out this claim. I move gradually from the theological center to the theological margins, from affirmations of the mystery, contingency, and goodness of the cosmic process, which have broad consensus in the Christian theological tradition, to affirmations of the graced and emergent nature of the cosmic process, which have a more ambivalent place, to affirmations of the non-anthropocentric and tragic structure of the cosmic process, which are deeply contested.

Queerer Than We Can Suppose: The Mystery of Cosmic Process

The cosmic process with which we are inextricably interwoven is mysterious, superabundant beyond our capacity to conceptualize or verbalize. It is composed of vast stretches of space and time that befuddle our animal brains, evolved as they are to navigate essentially human tribal scales. Science gives us inklings, predictive possibilities, and in local spheres even some measure of control over the mystery of the cosmic process. But beginnings and endings and expanses and depths remain beyond our grasp. We do not know the whence and whither of all things, and science can take us only so far with these limit questions. Even the most potent of our scientific theories is built upon probabilities and indeterminacies, and our understanding of beginnings and endings crashes up against singularities

---

4. See for example Brunner, *Justice and the Social Order*, 127–28.

in which language, even the language of mathematics, breaks down. In face of such mystery even scientists reach for speculative metaphysics. Perhaps we are the winners of a cosmic jackpot, our universe a bubble in the midst of an infinite sea of cosmic inflation. But such speculations do not seem far advanced beyond YHWH calling forth order out of the *tohu va vohu* of Genesis 1. They do not disperse the mystery of the cosmic process but rather affirm it. As J. B. S. Haldane famously said, not only is the universe "queerer than we suppose, but queerer than we can suppose."[5]

Of course Christians speak of the revelation of God in Jesus Christ, that this event or constellation of events shines in the darkness, illuminating our understandings of God, self, and world, making possible a faithful life *coram Deo*. Nevertheless, even given a robust affirmation of revelation, God remains *deus absconditus*, the creature (and not only the human creature) remains incommunicable and irreducibly other, and the cosmic process itself remains inexhaustibly mysterious.

"Let us not then seek assurance or finality," wrote Pascal. "Our reason is always deceived by the inconstancy of appearances; nothing can fix the finite which lies between the two infinities which enclose and flee from it . . . ."[6] We remain caught between infinities. This circumambient mystery evokes a sense of awe and wonder at the inexplicability of existence itself. It stands in contrast to reductionisms of any kind, whether a scientific reductionism that seeks to translate all things finally to equations and energy exchanges, or a theological reductionism that diminishes the abyssal mystery of the cosmic process by construing creation as an expendable bit player in the divine drama of human salvation. The mystery of cosmic process echoes the divine mystery, and the first and last word in both cases is silence.

Absolute Dependence: The Contingency of Cosmic Process

However, following Augustine, we must speak in order not to remain silent. The cosmic process is mysterious; it is also contingent—at least as rendered by Christian piety. Contingency entails an awareness of the absolute dependence of all things on the divine creativity. The cosmic process is not self-sustaining or self-explanatory. It is not necessary; it need not exist; it does not call itself into existence. Its sheer existence is gratuitous, and the

---

5. Haldane, *Possible Worlds*, 286.
6. Pascal, *Pensées*, 72.

pious mind perceives the overflowing creativity of the divine as the ground of the cosmic process.

Friedrich Schleiermacher, considered by some the "father of modern theology," sees here the very heart of Christian piety.[7] The feeling of absolute dependence stands in contrast to the feeling of relative dependence and relative freedom (or, together, reciprocity) we experience vis-à-vis other creatures and the entire causal nexus in which we are embedded. In relation to the causal nexus, we have some consciousness of being able to affect it (in however miniscule a way) and be affected by it. But in relation to God, the Whence of our existence, we have only consciousness of absolute dependence—or absolute divine causality, which is the same thing from the other side. This is not simply an affirmation of our "individual" absolute dependence. Because we are conscious of being part of the total causal nexus, that is, of existing in a relationship of reciprocity with the cosmic process, we are conscious of this entire causal nexus, this entire relation of reciprocity, as being absolutely dependent, as being contingent.

Every creature has as its ground of being, as the absolute cause of its existence, the divine causality—which, at the climax of his *Glaubenslehre*, Schleiermacher identifies as love.[8] God is love, which for Schleiermacher means the desire to be with and in the other. So the absolute ground of every creature's existence is this impartation of divine love—that is, divine immanence. For human creatures, the consciousness of being absolutely dependent (an affirmation of divine transcendence) is precisely the presence of absolute divine causality, that is, divine love (an affirmation of divine immanence). The consciousness of being absolutely dependent and the consciousness of being in relation to the divine love are one and the same in Christian piety.

Contingency points not only to the absolute dependence of the entire cosmic process on divine creativity, but also to the improbability and oddness of the particular structures of existence. As is commonly observed, if any of the fundamental forces that govern the interactions of matter had been even slightly different, the universe would be a wildly different place. The formation of stable nuclei requires a precise ratio between the strong nuclear and electromagnetic forces. A small change in their strengths could allow the electromagnetic force to overcome the strong nuclear force, and atoms could not exist. If electrons had any greater mass, they and protons

---

7. See for example Schleiermacher, *Christian Faith*, §4.3 and §4.4.
8. Ibid., §167.

would bond to form neutrons, disrupting the formation of heavy elements. If gravity were any stronger, stellar matter would bind more strongly and stars would use their fuel much faster, thus negating the possibility of the evolution of life. If gravity were any weaker, matter might not constellate to form larger structures, thus preventing the formation of stars in the first place.

Things seemingly could have been otherwise, cosmically and personally. The very conditions of human existence are fraught with near-incomprehensible improbabilities. Charles Darwin observed with amazement (and echoing Calvin in his own key):

> The world, it has often been remarked, appears as if it had long been preparing for the advent of man [sic]; and this, in one sense is strictly true, for he owes his birth to a long line of progenitors. If any single link in this chain had never existed, man would not have been exactly as he now is.[9]

Or as Bill Bryson more colorfully puts it:

> Consider the fact that for billions years, every one of your forebears on both sides has been attractive enough to find a mate, healthy enough to reproduce, and sufficiently blessed by fate and circumstances to live long enough to do so. Not one of your pertinent ancestors was squashed, devoured, drowned, starved, stranded, stuck fast, untimely wounded, or otherwise deflected from its life's quest of delivering a tiny charge of genetic material to the right partner at the right moment in order to perpetuate the only possible sequence of hereditary combinations that could result, eventually, astoundingly, and all too briefly—in you.[10]

The cosmic process itself, the emergence of trajectories conducive to human thriving and the emergence of particular individuals within each trajectory: each of these realities is suspended over an incomprehensible abyss of contingency. This contingency evokes a sense of dependence, a recognition that our very being is eccentric, centered outside itself. It also evokes for faith a sense of gratitude, a recognition that all the powers and processes and potentialities that brought us into being and sustain us in being are gifts. A sense of dependence decenters us and breaks us loose from the seemingly inevitable solipsism of the human condition. We do not and cannot create ourselves, hold ourselves in being, or determine our ultimate

---

9. Darwin, *Descent of Man*, 213.
10. Bryson, *Short History of Nearly Everything*, 3–4.

ends—much less can we do this for any other creature or for the cosmic process itself. And a sense of gratitude awakens us to the contingency and gratuity of other creatures, enabling us to see their fragile beauty, summoning us to wise and compassionate response.

"Sweetness in the Knowledge of It Alone": The Goodness of Cosmic Process

The cosmic process is good. This is a vital claim that the Christian theological tradition has generally sustained despite ever present temptations to dualistic visions that locate goodness in the soul over against the body or in a realm set apart from the dirtiness of physical reality. From the very first chapter of the book of Genesis, the goodness of creation, of the cosmic process, both in its constituent elements and its interconnected unity, is affirmed, and that affirmation has been consistently if at times tenuously maintained throughout the Christian theological tradition.

Of course the cosmic process is good *for us:* it has brought us into existence and given us space and time and potencies and potentialities. It has made it possible for one contingent creature to write these words and for other contingent creatures to read them. The cosmic process has been generative of all the goods we enjoy or can enjoy. This "goodness-for-us" evokes gratitude for divine gratuity. As John Calvin says in his commentary on Genesis 1:28:

> And hence we infer what was the end for which all things were created; namely, that none of the conveniences and necessities of life might be wanting to [humans]. In the very order of creation the paternal solicitude of God for [humans] is conspicuous, because [God] furnished the world with all things needful, and even with an immense profusion of wealth, before [God] formed [them]. Thus [humans were] rich before [they were] born.[11]

Below I will call into question Calvin's anthropocentrism, but for the moment he points us in the direction of a common affirmation of the Christian tradition: the cosmic process is good for us, not always and everywhere and for everyone, to be sure, but it is conducive to life and full of an abundance of good things necessary for creaturely thriving. This may not be the most significant sense in which the cosmic process is good, at least for my purposes

---

11. Calvin, *Calvin's Commentaries*, I:96.

here, but it *is* good in this sense, and failure to acknowledge it as such is to risk what can only be considered blasphemous cosmic ingratitude.

The cosmic process is good not only for us, that is, possessed of utilitarian goodness. It is also good in and for itself, that is, possessed of intrinsic goodness. The divine statement of goodness in Genesis 1 is given no grounding or utility. It is not good *for* this or that. It is not so much a divine declaration of goodness as a divine recognition of goodness, good-*seeing* speech rather than good-*making* speech. The cosmic process is good in itself. As a whole and in its constituent elements it has its own ends and its own life-before-God. As Terrence Fretheim has argued, the creation narrative of Genesis 1 suggests a divine engagement with the whole creative process, calling forth response and cooperation without coercive agency.[12] It is the seas and the lands that are the first creatures to respond to the divine call, long before human creatures have emerged. The life-before-God of the whole cosmic process rather dramatically precedes our own.

For Jonathan Edwards, the goodness of the cosmic process is connected to its harmony and proportion. "One alone, without any reference to any more, cannot be excellent; for in such a case there can be no matter of relation . . . and therefore, no such thing as consent."[13] The excellence or goodness of the cosmic process is tied to the harmony and proportion of consent among its related parts. Edwards's vision is essentially aesthetic. Cosmic process is good because it is beautiful.

Calvin even suggests that the purpose of the earth in the new creation is primarily aesthetic, that our contemplation of creation in the eschaton will be sublime beyond anything we have heretofore experienced because we will be able to contemplate it apart from our need of it: "in the very sight of it there will be such pleasantness, such sweetness in the knowledge of it alone, without the use of it, that this happiness will far surpass all the amenities that we now enjoy."[14]

Similarly, in the second vision of the first part of her *Scivias* Hildegard of Bingen suggests that Adam's original error was a failure of eros, a failure to take delight in all the trees of the garden. Or, as G. K. Chesterton wrote in "Ecclesiastes," "There is one sin—to call a green leaf gray."[15]

---

12. See Fretheim, *God and the World in the Old Testament*, chapter 2.
13. Edwards, *Scientific and Philosophical Writings*, 6:337.
14. Calvin, *Institutes*, 1006–7.
15. Chesterton, "Ecclesiastes," 310.

The goodness of the cosmic process is utilitarian (good for us), intrinsic, and aesthetic. It is also doxological. That is, it both praises the divine in the very expression of its fragile beauty, and it summons other creatures (most notably human creatures) to praise. As Calvin would put it, the cosmic process is good because it mirrors the glory of God.

> Correctly then is the world called the mirror of divinity, not that there is sufficient clearness for [humans] to gain a full knowledge of God by looking at the world, but... the faithful, to whom [God] has given eyes, see sparks of [God's] glory, as it were, glittering in every created thing. The world was no doubt made, that it might be the theater of divine glory.[16]

Calvin was neither the first nor the last to employ this image of the cosmic process as a theater of divine glory, but he employs it in an illuminating way. Instead of construing creation as a stage, with human beings as the primary actors and God as, in effect, the audience, Calvin puts God-in-creation on the stage. Human beings are the (admittedly benighted) audience, beholding the glory of God.

Calvin similarly uses pedagogical imagery: "then let the world become our school if we desire rightly to know God."[17] Thus we are called to meditate upon the cosmic process in order to deepen our discernment of God. But this schooling is not exclusively a schooling of the mind. The beauty and goodness of the cosmic process is a school of desire which awakens and redirects our longing for the divine.

> That we may enjoy the sight of God, [God] must come forth to view with [God's] clothing; that is to say, we must first cast our eyes upon the very beautiful fabric of the world in which [God] wishes to be seen by us.... [18]

> For in this world God blesses us in such a way as to give us a mere foretaste of [God's] kindness, and by that taste to entice us to desire heavenly blessings with which we may be satisfied.[19]

> As soon as we acknowledge God to be the supreme architect, who has erected the beauteous fabric of the universe, our minds must

---

16. Ibid., *Calvin's Commentaries*, XXII:266.
17. Ibid., I:57, 60.
18. Ibid., VI:145.
19. Ibid., *Calvin's New Testament Commentaries*, 10:244.

necessarily be ravished with wonder at [God's] infinite goodness, wisdom, and power.[20]

Calvin even alludes to the inevitability of divine judgment should we disrupt or deface the cosmic process:

> if we burn the book which our Lord has shown us, wittingly undermining the order [God] has established in nature by playing the butcher in killing the defenseless bird with our own hands—if we thereby prevent the bird from discharging its fatherly or motherly duty, then what will become of us?[21]

Perhaps even more significant, for Calvin the praise of God in and through the cosmic process is the very foundation of the world's stability. As he says, "if on earth such praise of God does not come to pass . . . then the whole order of nature will be thrown into confusion and creation will be annihilated."[22]

The cosmic process is good. Its goodness is utilitarian, intrinsic, aesthetic, and doxological. It is good for us and good in itself, with its own life-before-God. It is beautiful. It is a mirror of divine glory, a school of desire, and a summons to the praise of God.

A Cosmos of Grace: The Graced Nature of Cosmic Process

The cosmic process is good; it is also graced. If indeed the Creator is the Redeemer, as the Christian tradition has consistently maintained despite contestations with Gnostic and Marcionite impulses, then grace is not foreign to the world but embedded in it. Grace does not "[wait] upon the incarnation in Jesus Christ and then is explicated under a doctrine of redemption, but is also given with the ecological situation: prehuman, human, and in all other relations."[23] Grace is not simply or even primarily the act of God in overcoming the sinful estrangement of human beings. It is rather the "sheer givenness" or "primal givenness" of creation itself, the giftedness of being.[24]

> We may thus envision the nebula, galaxies, geospheres, biospheres, societies, and histories as a cosmos of grace, a region of gifts and

20. Ibid., *Calvin's Commentaries*, IV:309.
21. Quoted in Lane, *Ravished by Beauty*, 76.
22. Ibid., 66.
23. Sittler, *Evocations of Grace*, 86.
24. Ibid., 157.

occasions in which we encounter tendencies and trajectories of the Creator-Redeemer.[25]

The grace of cosmic process is indiscriminate; as Jesus says, God causes the sun to shine and the rain to fall on the just and the unjust (Matt 5:45). It is the overflowing superabundance of possibility and fecundity; the grace of redemption is but a chapter of this larger story.

Of course Calvin would argue that God's preserving or general grace is universally present to fallen creation, restraining the worst consequences of sin (i.e., the second use of the law), preserving natural order, and maintaining historical and cultural life from complete disintegration. But we must go deeper than that. The entire cosmic process is graced. To be is to be a manifestation of grace, the overflowing gratuity of the divine. Once again this perspective evokes gratitude and prompts a decentering of the human creature, and it stands in contrast to any perspective that puts history in opposition to nature, or looks to nature as either simply raw material for human development or the stage upon which the human-divine drama of redemption plays out.

Three Big Bangs: The Emergence of Cosmic Process

The cosmic process is dynamic and evolving. It is shaped by emergence, that is, by the appearance of novel properties that cannot be explained simply by reference to their constituent elements. "The properties of a rose, or any other living organism, cannot be interpreted on the basis of atoms and molecules."[26] Water has properties that neither oxygen nor hydrogen possess.

Emergence occurs at both macro and micro levels. One could tell the entire story of the cosmic process as the story of three great emergents— "three big bangs" in Holmes Rolston's phrase[27]: the emergence of matter-energy beginning some 13.7 billion years ago (the first "big bang"); the emergence of life beginning some 3 billion years ago; and the emergence of mind beginning some 200,000 years ago. The emergence of matter-energy makes possible the beauty of form, proportion, harmony, and contrast, evoking senses of awe, wonder, and desire. With the emergence of life there

---

25. Ottati, *Theology for Liberal Protestants*, 177.
26. Luisi, *Emergence of Life*, 119.
27. Rolston, *Three Big Bangs*.

are possibilities for sociality, kinship, empathy, and conflict: the reality of the other as both lure and threat. The action of mirroring neurons draws creatures out of solipsism and toward relationship, synthesis, cooperation, and novelty.[28] And with the emergence of mind comes the possibility of love (perhaps an intensification of empathy), not only feeling the pain or pleasure of another creature but actively seeking to be "with and in the other" (as Schleiermacher has it), engaging higher levels of consciousness, reflexivity, thought, and imagination.

Matter-energy, life, mind—beauty, life, love—these are emergent properties of a complexly nested cosmic process. They can be distinguished but not separated, and they do not easily succumb to hierarchical ordering. The cosmic process is not chaos; there are orderings, to be sure. Many of these orderings take on accretions of social construction and distortion, and so we must be very careful not to ascribe particular social constructions to "nature," especially given that "nature" itself is in process. But we also cannot deny certain fundamental ordering processes that make emergence possible, and we violate those orderings at our peril. (As I will suggest below, this may be a way of retrieving theological language of divine judgment in our context.) At the same time, the cosmic process is ordered but by no means a fixed order, as has at times been claimed with deeply destructive consequences, holding this or that socially constructed and sinfully distorted order to be *the* "natural" or "God-given" order. It is a dynamic ordering, an emergent process in constant flux. Beauty and life and love provide touchstones, points of orientation, but the cosmic process flows ever on.

A Place and a Time: The Non-Anthropocentricity of Cosmic Process

The cosmic process is not centered on the human creature. In some ways this should be a commonplace observation. What has science been but a series of dislocations and demotions of the human animal? Copernicus removed the earth from center stage; Darwin downgraded the human animal from the hand-crafted child of God, "a little lower than the angels" (Ps. 8:5), to a mere drop in an ongoing stream of evolutionary struggle. Contemporary cosmology has expanded the cosmic horizon beyond the capacity of our imagination. Carl Sagan summarizes our modern sense of place:

28. See for example Rizzolatti and Craighero, "The mirror-neuron system."

> We live on a hunk of rock and metal that orbits a humdrum star in the obscure outskirts of an ordinary galaxy comprised of 400 billion stars in a universe of some hundred billion galaxies, which may be one of a very large number, perhaps an infinite number of separate, closed-off universes. Many, perhaps most, of those stars probably have planets. In this perspective, how can anyone seriously believe that we are central—physically, much less to the purpose of the universe?[29]

"When I look at your heavens, the work of your fingers, the moon and the stars that you have established; what are human beings that you are mindful of them, mortals that you care for them?" (Ps 8:3–4).

Of course the testimony of the Old Testament to the place of the human creature in the midst of creation is multifaceted. Looking at the various creation narratives (William Brown reminds us that there are at least seven creation stories[30]), we see a complex range of affirmations: the human creature is both in the "image of God" (Gen 1:26–27) and made from the earth (Gen 2:7, 19), and the call to dominion is interwoven with the call to sabbath rest and service. As we have seen, Psalm 8 both affirms the vastness of creation and yet the particular elevation of the human creature. Psalm 104 and Job 38–41 both embed the human creature more fully in the cosmic process itself: human beings have a time and a place in creation, but that time and place is delicately balanced with the time and place of other creatures. Humans thrive in the day while lions take the night (Ps 104:19–23), and the human place is but a small clearing in an encompassing wilderness in which God delights (Job 38–41).

Yet there has been a tendency in Christian theological reflection to smooth out the rougher, more textured testimony of the text, to extricate the affirmations of human exceptionalism from the affirmations of human embeddedness. The work of Philip Rolnick is an instructive example. I engage Rolnick at some length because he is a contemporary theologian fully cognizant of the contestations surrounding affirmations of human uniqueness. He helpfully illustrates both the promise and perils of theological anthropocentrism.

In *Person, Grace, and God*, Rolnick articulates an understanding of the human person that intends to stand in continuity with the deepest insights

---

29. Sagan's speech on the occasion of his sixtieth birthday, in Terzian and Bilson, *Carl Sagan's Universe*, 148.

30. Brown, *Seven Pillars of Creation*.

of the Christian theological tradition and to respond to, without being overcome by, challenges from contemporary science and postmodern thought. He navigates the choppy waters of evolutionary biology, arguing that the self-regard endemic to all biological entities is a gift of God—being is good and so the desire to continue being is good—but that this self-regard must be construed through Christ, such that "the spiritual technique of self-love is other-love."[31] And while valuing the postmodern penchant for breaking open totalizing systems, Rolnick rejects its presumed nihilism and denial of transcendence, arguing that "decentering the modernist self terminates an illusion, but if nothing then takes the center, two interrelated options become likely: self-spillage unto the *nihil* or power sought for self-assertion. Running directly counter to postmodernist trends, the relation to God as center positions us in the grandest of grand narratives, wherein persons are dynamically oriented by faith."[32]

Placing God at the center of this "grandest of grand narratives" effectively places personality at the center, for this is the triune God (three persons in one nature), the God who became incarnate in Christ (two natures in one person), a God whose gift to human animals is personality. The ethical and theological implications of this centering on the personal are profound and ambiguous. Rolnick is able to make sense out of the human person through the many toils and snares of biology and postmodernism; he is able to integrate the human person with the theological center of the Christian tradition; and his notion of personality as *incommunicabilis* is suggestive of a profound ethic. However, Rolnick's consistent restriction of personality to human animals (in addition to the triune God and angels) is ethically and theologically problematic, and leads to an impoverishment of creation and ultimately of God.

Rolnick's primary task is a daunting one: to define the indefinable. Personality is a gift of God and shares in God's irreducible mystery. Rolnick takes different approaches to naming this mystery. At times he proceeds *via negativa*: "the task before us is to communicate the incommunicable, to articulate a reality that cannot be understood as a definite essence, cannot be understood solely as a web of relations, even though relationship is absolutely vital to personality, and cannot be understood as psychological tendencies. Personality is no thing; nor is it nothing."[33] Lest he be reduced

---

31. Rolnick, *Person, Grace, and God*, 86.
32. Ibid., 122.
33. Ibid., 211.

to silence, at other times Rolnick lists characteristics or capacities that seem to be marks of personality, though he is quite clear that personality cannot be reduced to any of these "whats": unity, freedom, dignity, will, intelligence, relationality.[34] Perhaps most significant among these "whats" is self-transcendence, which Rolnick calls the *sine qua non* of "the divine gift of personality."[35] Likewise he argues that "to deny or denigrate a unique and unrepeatable self-consciousness is to deny the inner engine of the divine gift of personality."[36]

Perhaps Rolnick's primary rubric for talking about personality is *incommunicabilis*, that is, the nontransferable uniqueness of the person. Nature is shared, transferable; personality is not. Personality is always more than nature, a "who" not a "what."[37] Personality may be dependent upon nature—you cannot have a nature-less person—but it ultimately transcends nature.

> The resilience of the subject/person, even to the most severe interrogation, implies that, even though persons are entirely incarnate in nature, culture, and history, something in persons always rises beyond the calculable, predictable, and understandable, like Jesus' parable of the yeast hidden within the flour.[38]

This understanding of the irreducible mystery, transcendence, incommunicability, and non-transference of personality has important ethical implications. The "who" that can never be reduced to a "what" can never be fully subsumed into a larger narrative. Personality (who-ness) is a divine gift that cannot be completely absorbed into another's subjectivity, and thus cannot be possessed by another, cannot be reduced to a "what." When encountering a person one is always encountering an other, one who makes (Emmanuel Levinas would say infinite) ethical demands.

Regrettably, Rolnick is quite consistent in restricting personality to human animals. Many nonhuman creatures are mentioned in the text—bees, trees, fishes, stones, ducks, for example—but in each case the intent is to distinguish between human animals as persons and nonhumans as nonpersons. Even in cases where human persons are not explicitly juxtaposed with nonhuman nonpersons, the implication seems clear. When discussing

34. Ibid., 208–9.
35. Ibid., 214.
36. Ibid., 212.
37. Ibid., 8.
38. Ibid., 120.

incommunicabilis, for example, Rolnick notes that atoms are interchangeable, while human personality is not. True—however, he skips over a rather large sampling of biological possibilities. Atoms may be interchangeable, but are trees? Is it the case, to paraphrase the former governor of California, that "a tree's a tree; if you've seen one, you've seen them all"? Or is there something incommunicable, nontransferable, about this particular tree in this particular place and time, something non-repeatable and non-interchangeable—dare I say, something personal?

Rolnick consistently averts this possibility, even when it seems near the surface. For example:

> The finite is not a failure, lack, or deprivation. It is gloriously new. It is creation. For all who are not God, it is a pathway to life, a summons and invitation to participate in an utterly new expression of divine being, the unfolding drama from the putative big bang to the moment in which I write and you read this very sentence.[39]

This dramatic vision seems promising, until one remembers the strict distinction between "who" (person) and "what" (nature). Only human animals can be persons, so only human animals are invited to participate in this drama.

Of course that overstates the case. All creation certainly has a role to play in this drama, but the role of nonhumans is primarily (or exclusively) instrumental. Rolnick quotes Thomas Langford approvingly: "The whole creation is so ordered as to develop, try, mature, and enrich man's self-determination and fulfillment of moral personhood."[40] Rolnick certainly stands in good company in claiming that creation is ordered primarily toward human good—arguably he has most of the tradition at his side—but there are troubling implications of this claim. Instrumentalism seems inextricably linked with anthropocentrism (or, perhaps better, theanthropocentrism). After considering the seemingly "anthropic" dimensions of cosmic evolution, Rolnick quips, "It may be anthropocentric to say that humanity is the chief purpose of evolution, but it may also be right."[41] Perhaps most telling: "The person who can receive the divine gift (grace) is more valuable than the whole universe, because the universe is a what, not a who, and the what exists for the sake of the who."[42] It is difficult to know what to make of this

39. Ibid., 173.
40. Ibid., 223.
41. Ibid., 77.
42. Ibid., 169.

breathtaking claim. At the very least it seems clear that Rolnick has forcefully upheld an affirmation of human exceptionalism, but in the process the rest of the cosmic process has been left behind.

Granted, my suggestion that the category of personhood might be expanded to include other-than-human creatures may jeopardize the specificity and theological utility of the concept. If everything is personal, nothing is personal. There may be ways to use the category of personhood to indicate something distinct about the human creature while utilizing other conceptualities to bring other-than-human creatures into the theological circle. Similar to Rolnick, in *Difference and Identity: A Theological Anthropology*, Ian A. McFarland uses the concept of personhood (shorn of essentialism and pure constructivism) to point to distinctively human possibilities (made possible "by virtue of God's action toward us in Christ," to be sure[43]). But as he turns to the "symptoms" of being human, symptoms which point in the direction of a human nature only realized eschatologically, the first such symptom is the call for humans to have "dominion" in Genesis 1.[44] McFarland is quick to note that dominion can and must be interpreted christologically: cruciform dominion would not be power-over but rather suffering-with. McFarland restricts personhood to the human creature (as does Rolnick) but then identifies the first symptom of being human as relating to the other-than-human world. Whether or not McFarland's approach is finally satisfactory, it demonstrates that the concept of personhood restricted to the human creature need not result in the kind of bracketing out of the other-than-human that we see in Rolnick.

Nevertheless, Rolnick clearly represents an anthropocentric tendency that has long characterized Christian theology. This kind of theological anthropocentrism was one of the primary targets of Lynn White's famous 1967 *Science* article, "The Historical Roots of Our Ecological Crisis." White may have been right in his critique, but wrong in his implication that this was the sum total of the Christian witness. There are undoubtedly counter-testimonies in the tradition. In *The Travail of Nature: The Ambiguous Ecological Promise of Christian Theology*, Paul Santmire, for example, sees ecologically promising trajectories in thinkers such as Irenaeus, Augustine, Aquinas, and Bonaventure. White himself saw Francis of Assisi as modeling an alternative path. In any case, it seems clear that Christian theology has at times struggled to shake its anthropocentric addiction.

43. McFarland, *Difference and Identity*, 72.
44. Ibid., 149.

> There is something wrong with our world view. It is still Ptolemaic, though the sun is no longer believed to revolve around the earth. We see ourselves as the culmination and the end, and if we do indeed consider our passing, we think that sunlight will go with us and the earth be dark. We are the end. For us continents rose and fell, for us the waters and the air were mastered, for us the great living web has pulsated and grown more intricate.[45]

In my judgment it is simply not credible to observe the vastness of cosmic process, the scales of time and space involved, to observe the roiling fecundity of the evolving biosphere, and to conclude that human animals are the center and meaning of the whole process. It is incredible—and it is dangerous, because it permits value judgments that put the thriving of human creatures over the entire rest of the cosmic process. If, as Rolnick suggested, a person "who can receive the divine gift . . . is more valuable than the whole universe," how does this shape or misshape our ethical orientation toward the other-than-human world?[46]

These are delicate matters, to be sure, for charges of anthropocentrism are often followed by countercharges of misanthropy or ecofascism. Theological anthropology has always traced subtle lines of continuity and discontinuity between human creatures and nonhuman creatures. Generally the lines of discontinuity have been the most theologically significant—what sets human creatures apart from the rest of creation—and the doctrine of *imago Dei* has often been used as the marker of this "set apartness." Whatever human creatures may share with nonhuman creatures, *imago Dei* marks their differentiation, whether the differentiating factor is understood as reason or freedom or self-consciousness or transcendence or capacity for communion with God or personality in Rolnick's sense, etc.

This affirmation of differentiation and discontinuity has become more complex in contemporary theology, as we now have greater awareness of the biological and evolutionary processes that brought human creatures and all other living creatures into existence. We are also increasingly aware of the (at least rudimentary) presence in nonhuman creatures of many characteristics that were once used as markers of human differentiation.

Ultimately we must affirm that human creatures are embedded within and yet in some sense transcendent of the natural processes that brought them into existence. Langdon Gilkey reminds us that the word *nature* is

---

45. Eiseley, *Immense Journey*, 57.
46. Rolnick, *Person, Grace, and God*, 239.

used in both senses, to indicate the total matrix of which we are a part and also to differentiate human animals from nonhuman nature (i.e., juxtaposing nature and culture).[47] A failure to affirm human continuity with and embeddedness in nature risks creating a destructive dualism that cuts human creatures off from the rest of creation, ultimately draining creation of value and meaning and rendering human existence unintelligible. Yet a failure to affirm human discontinuity from nature risks collapsing into a "monistic materialism"[48] that denies the unique capacities and responsibilities of the human creature. The challenge is to hold the affirmations of exceptionalism and embeddedness together.

Process thought has its own way of both honoring the distinctive value of human animals and so allowing judgments of relative value to be made without inscribing those into absolute dualisms. If the end of creative process is the enjoyment of beauty, as Whitehead suggests, then a creature with a greater capacity to enjoy such beauty contributes more to the ongoing process. A human being has relatively more creative power and freedom for enjoyment of beauty than a beetle; therefore one can be justified in putting a human life ahead of a beetle. This valuation is troubling to many ecological ethicists and animal rights activists alike, and it is not unproblematic. While this may be an advance on qualitative distinctions between humans and other creatures, it can be excessively individualistic and inattentive to the importance of ecosystems. A worm is less interesting than a bird (and thus less intrinsically valuable from a process perspective), but without worms the birds die.[49]

There are other ways to affirm distinct human possibilities and responsibilities in the midst of a non-anthropocentric cosmos from a process perspective. Actual occasions are the fundamental elements of reality, and all living entities (human or otherwise) will be successions or societies of such actual occasions. Thus the differentiation between humans and

---

47. Langdon Gilkey points to two interrelated meanings of nature: "On the one hand, nature is represented in both archaic religion and modern science as the all-encompassing source or ground of all there is in concrete experience: the entities, inorganic and organic; the system of nature; ourselves; and even historical communities are products of nature.... Nature as a word, a concept, a symbol, signals on the other hand our distinction from, even our distance from, this environment." "Nature" refers both to the total matrix of which human beings are a part and to that which is in some sense distinguishable from history and culture. See Gilkey, *Nature, Reality, and the Sacred*, 178-79.

48. Barth's term in *Church Dogmatics*, III/2, 382.

49. Sideris, *Environmental Ethics*, 121.

nonhumans is not ontological. Both are shaped by the same dynamics of actual occasions, prehension, concrescence, and so forth. The differentiation made possible by process thought is a quantitative rather than a qualitative differentiation. Human beings may be capable of greater complexity, greater intensity, greater harmony of contrasts in their becoming—and this is not an insignificant claim, particularly when it comes to ethical determinations vis-à-vis other forms of life. But there is no ontological basis for separating humans from nonhumans in their communion with the world—or with the divine. To reemphasize this last point, in process thought all actual occasions, whether they constitute human or nonhuman societies, stand in principle in the same relationship of communion with God. Thus a process thinker is able to affirm discontinuity in a quantitative rather than a qualitative mode that permits ethical differentiation without necessarily creating destructive hierarchies.

Can we consent to a cosmic process in which we participate but which is not centered on us? We have had occasion to consider Psalm 104 already. Human beings have their niche in the divine ecology. They have their place and their time. But so do all the other creatures in the roll of creation. The lions have their place and time. Every creature has its life-with-others and its life-before-God. The one place in Psalm 104 where humans might be said to have a unique capacity is in v. 35. Human beings have the capacity to sin, to disrupt the fragile interconnection of all the creatures of a given system and perhaps even threaten the integrity of God's good creation.

There is no denying that the human animal is marked by particular possibilities and therefore particular responsibilities. But those possibilities and responsibilities are local in scale. Romans 8 may rightly point to the potential of human sinfulness to disrupt the life systems of the earth, but this is not to say that creation, or the cosmic process itself, can be disrupted by human agency. "Christ plays in ten thousand places," divine creativity unfolds in a thousand thousand more. Human agency has a place and a time, and in that place and time we have much to be and to do and to become. But there are other trajectories unfolding, and even if we finally succeed in the destruction of our own trajectory, the cosmic process continues. Or, as Moltmann says: "the song of praise was sung before the appearance of human beings, is sung outside the sphere of human beings, and will be sung even after human beings have (perhaps) disappeared from this planet."[50]

---

50. Moltmann, *God in Creation*, 197.

Perpetual Perishing:
The Tragic Structure of Cosmic Process

Perhaps the greatest challenge in articulating an understanding of the cosmic process interpreted through the lens of the Christian theological and scriptural tradition might be called the problem of perpetual perishing. The concept of "perpetual perishing" can be traced from Heraclitus to Locke to Whitehead.[51] It is the river one cannot step into twice. "Time, like an ever rolling stream/soon bears us all away." Following Whitehead, Schubert Ogden defines it as "the inevitable transience of all our moments of experience," the perishing of all actual occasions as they achieve satisfaction.[52]

It is the perpetual perishing of all the constituent elements of the cosmic process that is relevant for our purposes, and one need not be a Whiteheadian or an existentialist to see that, while Tennyson's "nature, red in tooth and claw" tells only part of the story, the part it tells is true. It is certainly the case, as ecological theologians often emphasize, that nature is interdependent, but interdependence does not always indicate harmony or community. Nothing is more interdependent than the food chain. The natural world bequeathed to us by Darwin is a world of struggle, predation, parasitism, and death—not exclusively, but overwhelmingly. Nature is perpetual perishing.

Further, perpetual perishing is the *sine qua non* for creative advance (to borrow Whitehead's terminology again). Life feeds on death. It is fuel for the evolutionary process, the chisel by which natural selection carves new forms of life. As Holmes Rolston says, "The cougar's fang sharpens the deer's sight, the deer's fleet-footedness shapes a more supple lioness . . . ."[53] Without predation, pain, struggle, and death, without perpetual perishing, the complexity of life becomes unimaginable.

> The animal skills demanded [in a world without predation] would be only a fraction of those that have resulted in actual zoology—no horns, no fleet-footed predators or prey, no fine-tuned eyesight and hearing, no quick neural capacity, no advanced brains.[54]

---

51. See for example Whitehead, *Process and Reality,* 29, 60, 146–47.
52. Ogden, *Reality of God,* 224.
53. Rolston, "Perpetual Perishing, Perpetual Renewal," 111.
54. Rolston, "Disvalues in Nature," 254.

Much of what we value, not the least our very existence, emerges from the perpetual perishing of nature: "beauty forged out of suffering."[55]

As Gary Snyder reminds us:

> Life in the wild is not just eating berries in the sunlight. I like to imagine a "depth ecology" that would go to the dark side of nature—the ball of crunched bones in a scat, the feathers in the snow, the tales of insatiable appetite. Wild systems are in one elevated sense above criticism, but they can also be seen as irrational, moldy, cruel, parasitic . . . . Life is not just a diurnal property of large interesting vertebrates; it is also nocturnal, anaerobic, cannibalistic, microscopic, digestive, fermentative: cooking away in the warm dark.[56]

It is this seeming negativity at the very heart of natural processes that poses such a stark challenge for theology. How might we locate the divine in the warm dark? How might God dwell in and with a nature that is moldy, parasitic, digestive, fermentative, deathly?

Theologians deploy various strategies to protect the divine from contamination by such negativities. At times even ecologically minded theologians construe a sanitized deity in a sanitized nature by overemphasizing interdependence interpreted as harmony to the neglect of competition, struggle, and death. However, if we intend to theologize about the cosmic process as it is, and not a romantic facsimile thereof, if we intend to be shaped by what science tells us about natural processes, if we intend to view nature with a "loving eye" as opposed to an "arrogant eye"[57]—we cannot ignore the reality of perpetual perishing.

We also cannot ascribe it to a primordial "fall" through which an otherwise-harmonious creation is plunged into predatory conflict by human sin. Though this trope is well-attested in the tradition—Calvin, for example, argues in his commentary on Genesis that the fall made previously tame animals savage—contemporary science has rendered such an explanation incredible. Predators and parasites predate the arrival of *Homo sapiens*. "Long before humans arrived, the way of nature was already a *via dolorosa*."[58] Despite its presence in the tradition, the notion of a primordial "fall" as an explanation for the reality of perpetual perishing blinds us not

---

55. Southgate, *Groaning of Creation*, 55.
56. Snyder, "Blue Mountains Constantly Walking," 118.
57. See McFague, *Body of God*, chapter 2.
58. Rolston, "Kenosis and Nature," 60.

only to science but also to the inherent ambiguity of nature itself. Might it blind us to the inherent ambiguity of the divine nature as well?[59]

A far more prevalent but no less problematic possibility is to eschew the "fall" as etiology and focus instead on the garden as eschatology (as we saw with Moltmann). That is, instead of imagining an Edenic harmony from which nature fell, we imagine an Edenic eschatology toward which nature moves (or is drawn). But this theological landscaping—relocating the garden from the front to the back of the theological house—creates its own challenges, for if our eschatological vision is predicated on the cessation of perpetual perishing ("death will be no more"), it envisions not the redemption of nature but the end of nature, nature defanged and declawed, tamed and humanized. In the eschatological extirpation of the evolutionary tares from the ecological wheat, nature may be "redeemed" only by being "transformed"—that is, denatured.

In a sermon on Job, Calvin speaks of the "order of nature which is like a mirror in which we are able to contemplate that which is of God."[60] Of course Calvin also thought of nature as fallen, so the mirror was cracked and blurred, along with our capacity to see it properly. Leaving aside the "fall" trope for a moment, we are left with perhaps a radical possibility: that the cosmic process as it is, not as it was or as it will be, the cosmic process as creative advance through perpetual perishing—that precisely *this* mirrors the divine glory.

The cosmic process, then, is tragically structured. This tragic structure is not the result of a cataclysmic fall, nor is it a deficiency endemic to an incomplete creation that will one day be overcome. The cosmic process is good but it is so ordered that suffering is inevitable. Embodiment opens up channels of both pleasure and pain; diversity allows for both cooperation and competition; finitude is the fuel of novelty but also of loss, decay, and death.

Suffering is inevitable, but not absolute. Wendy Farley[61] looks to compassion as an empowering power that draws us into real relation with those who suffer, awakening us to their reality and their beauty, summoning us to justice and healing. This compassion is grounded in the divine compassion. The tragically structured world is not the result of indifferent or

---

59. For a bracing and unsettling reflection along this trajectory, see Carroll, *Savage Side*.

60. Quoted in Schreiner, *Theater of His Glory*, 107.

61. See Farley, *Tragic Vision and Divine Compassion*.

malevolent powers. It is ordered by and toward Divine Eros. However, if creation is ordered toward the impartation of divine love (Schleiermacher), if creation is ordered toward the intensification of experience and the creation of beauty (Whitehead), then suffering is an inevitable concomitant of creation. Creatures able to receive and share love are also able to endure and inflict pain. Creatures able to create beauty are also able to destroy beauty. Beauty itself is a fragile harmony of contrasts full of pathos.

The cosmic process in which we are embedded is mysterious and contingent. It is good—good for us, good in itself, aesthetically good, doxologically good—and it is graced. It is evolving and emerging and dynamic. It is not centered on the human animal, though the human animal has a place and a time within it, and it is tragically structured, creative advance through perpetual perishing, with the very goods of creaturely existence entailing suffering.

When we take our stand on the bit of dirt beneath our feet, when we commit ourselves to solidarity with the dust and, by that, solidarity with the entire interconnected web of existence, when we embrace humility, it is *this* cosmic process and no other—this beautiful and broken, graced and grieving creation that God so loves—to which we finally consent.

5

"What Beauty Is For"

Hope and the Efficacy of Beauty

Did you too see it, drifting, all night, on the black river?
Did you see it in the morning, rising into the silvery air—
An armful of white blossoms,
A perfect commotion of silk and linen as it leaned
into the bondage of its wings; a snowbank, a bank of lilies,
Biting the air with its black beak?
Did you hear it, fluting and whistling
A shrill dark music—like the rain pelting the trees—like a waterfall
Knifing down the black ledges?
And did you see it, finally, just under the clouds—
A white cross Streaming across the sky, its feet
Like black leaves, its wings Like the stretching light of the river?
And did you feel it, in your heart, how it pertained to everything?
And have you too finally figured out what beauty is for?
And have you changed your life?

—Mary Oliver, "The Swan"

John Calvin reminds us that "without knowledge of self there is no knowledge of God." He might well have added "knowledge of the world." These three—God, self, and world—constitute "nearly all the wisdom we possess" and are "joined by many bonds."[1] What we say about one decisively shapes

---

1. Calvin, *Institutes*, 35.

what we may say about the others. For just this reason Calvin is quite clear that we must begin, not with the world or the self, but with God, if we are not to go astray. With apologies to Calvin, I have worked the other direction. I began with a discussion of "world"—the cosmic process to which we consent in humility—because it is precisely this term that occupies such an ambivalent and contested place in theological reflection, and also because the loss of this term not only distorts our understanding of God and self (as Calvin knew well) but also fuels (or at least fails to curtail) a destructive disregard toward nature.

As we turn from humility to hope, reflections on God become more central. This is not to say that "world" is left behind; quite the contrary. Just as I could not explore the dynamics of cosmic process without noting its absolute dependence on divine creativity or the ways in which the human self is inextricably embedded within it, so I cannot explore the dynamics of hope born of divine beauty without also examining the self or the world that is responsive to or expressive of such beauty. To echo Calvin, all three terms are "joined by many bonds."

Nevertheless, as we turn to a discussion of hope, the center of gravity does shift toward the first term (God). No doubt there are grounds for hope in the fecundity of cosmic process and in the resiliency of ecosystems. But as for the endurance of the human meaning that has been interwoven with cosmic process, or for the hundreds or even thousands of species that go extinct every year, the fecundity and resilience of cosmic process provides little succor.

Surely there are grounds for hope in the human capacity to adapt, to be roused to ethical action. Regrettably this ethical action is typically motivated by self-interest, whether in "light green" anthropocentric and utilitarian ethical approaches or even "dark green" ecocentric approaches that encourage one to expand one's sense of self to be inclusive of ecosystems, such as in deep ecology.[2] Granting that there is a sense in which organisms are rightly ordered toward self-interest and self-preservation, nevertheless human beings have the capacity to explode this natural self-interest into regimes of rapacious destructiveness. What hope is there to be found in human ethical action when it is grounded in self-interest and so deeply distorted by concupiscence? What is necessary for the self to respond to the

---

2. For a discussion of "light green" and "dark green" ecological ethics, see Curry, *Ecological Ethics*. Curry's use of "dark green" overlaps somewhat with Bron Taylor's, though Taylor places greater emphasis on radical environmentalism and the "shadow side" of dark green ethics. See Taylor, *Dark Green Religion*.

fragile beauty of the other, or to the divine beauty that lures the self into an eccentric existence of self-giving love?

In what follows I will be pursuing the question of hope, weaving around the three terms of God, self, and world. God is "the hope of all the ends of the earth and of the farthest sea" (Ps 65:5b). That hope manifests itself in both judgment and redemption. But it takes root only in a redeemed self, that is, a self that has relinquished its grasp on the idols of proximate goods and has been set free from endlessly destructive strategies for self-securing, a self that has been founded in God. This self can hope. This self can be an agent (and not merely a patient) in the ongoing judging and redeeming work of God. This self can respond to beauty. And that is where our hope is finally to be found: in beauty, the fragile beauty of each creature that evokes wonder and compassion, the beauty of a redeemed self set free to go out in love for the other, and the beauty of God that draws all creation along trajectories of beauty and life and love.

Hope in Judgment and Redemption

God is active in all things as judge and redeemer. It is God we have to do with in all events, conditions, and relations of our lives. In all things God is active as both limit and possibility, form and dynamic (to borrow Tillich's polarity). I take this affirmation of the divine judging and redeeming activity in and through all things to be central to the Reformed tradition in which I stand. Of course for Calvin it takes the form of exhaustive divine sovereignty and particular providence: every drop of rain falls by divine determination and every babe nurses or fails to nurse by divine intent. I am not inclined to follow Calvin in this interpretation given the tangled nest of questions it raises with regard to scientific causality, human freedom and responsibility, evil and suffering, and anthropomorphic conceptions of the divine. I follow instead H. Richard Niebuhr (also standing in the Reformed tradition), who speaks of God as the dynamic "structure of the universe" or the "creative will" that is both the "rock against which we beat in vain" and the "source of all meaning."[3]

The dialectic of judgment and redemption is central not only to the Reformed tradition. It also reflects the "christomorphic" structure of Christian thought. The judging and redeeming activity of God in the narratives of crucifixion and resurrection forms a *gestalt* through which Christians

3. Niebuhr, "The Only Way Into the Kingdom," 15.

interpret the events, conditions, and relations of their lives. For example, Niebuhr speaks of Christ as the "symbolic form" through which we perceive the activity of God in both history and nature.[4] He explores how the cross, not simply as historical event but as "a revelation of the order of reality," illuminates the tragic mystery of the Second World War:

> If the Son of God is being crucified in this war along with the malefactors—and he is being crucified on many an obscure hill—then the graciousness of God, the self-giving love, is more manifest here than in all the years of peace.[5]

It is only by faith in resurrection that Niebuhr is able "to find hope along with brokenheartedness in the midst of disaster."[6]

This same "christomorphic" reasoning can be found in Niebuhr's reflections on nature: "It [divine love] has created fellowship in atoms and organisms, at bitter cost to electrons and cells; and it is creating something better than human selfhood but at bitter cost to that selfhood."[7] Here Niebuhr alludes to what environmental ethicist Holmes Rolston calls the "cruciformity" of nature:

> The enigmatic symbol of the cross . . . is a parable of all natural and cultural history. . . . We cannot take this Garden Earth as paradise in which there was neither labor nor pain; even in the Garden Earth, life has to be redeemed in the midst of perpetual perishing. The Garden Earth forebodes the Garden of Gethsemane. Creation is cruciform.[8]

This dialectic of judgment and redemption is also central to the Old Testament prophetic tradition. Ronald Clements has argued that, despite the varying historical exigencies of the prophets, the texts have been shaped by the canonical process such that a clear pattern emerges.

> The place where both aspects [the coming judgment and the salvation of Israel] are brought together is to be found in the structure of the canonical collection of prophecy; the threat of doom is

---

4. Niebuhr, *Responsible Self*, 154–59.
5. Niebuhr, "War As Crucifixion," 28–29.
6. Niebuhr, "War As the Judgment of God," 23.
7. Niebuhr, "The Only Way Into the Kingdom", 16.
8. Rolston, "Does Nature Need to Be Redeemed?," 221.

followed by the word of salvation, which does not evade the judgment but looks beyond it.[9]

Judgment and redemption form the paradigmatic pattern of divine activity in the prophetic canon.

We see this same dialectic at work in Tillich's discussion of the *kairos*. A *kairos* is a moment in the historical process in which the absolute appears to the relative as "judgment and creation," where "the eternal breaks into the temporal, shaking and transforming it and creating a crisis in the depth of human existence."[10] While for Christian faith the *kairos* refers preeminently to the coming of Jesus as the Christ, in its general sense the *kairos* is "every turning-point in history in which the eternal judges and transforms the temporal."[11] This is suggestive of a "kairotic dialectic," a divine Yes-and-No, a judging and redeeming movement. I am persuaded that our escalating ecological crisis is a *kairos* in Tillich's sense, and so it becomes incumbent upon interpreters, shaped by this dialectic, to discern the Yes-and-No, the divine judging and redeeming activity in the fullness of time.

Hope is rooted in such discernment. It is an affirmation of what may be the elemental expression of faith, the conviction that we are not alone, that there are other powers and processes at work in the world for good. I certainly agree with Edward Farley that the actuality of redemption is the first moment in theological reflection.[12] But I believe that the category of judgment, contested and distorted though it may be, can also evoke hope, because it is an affirmation divine engagement, divine presence, even if that presence is presently experienced as judgment, as "no."

Is it potentially redemptive to construe species loss, acidifying oceans, deteriorating food chains, violent and unpredictable weather, and so on, not simply as the inevitable by-products of excessive CO_2 emissions but also as divine judgment? If creation is God's primal covenant partner, God's "first love," the first creature to hear and respond to the divine word ("Let there be . . . "), and if the human creature has been doing violence to that covenant partner for centuries, is it beyond the faithful imagination to contemplate divine judgment, even divine wrath? If we construe our ecological crisis as divine judgment, rather than simply the inexorable flow of natural processes, perhaps instead of evoking responses of technological

---

9. Clements, "Patterns of the Prophetic Canon," 55.
10. Tillich, "Kairos," 38, 45.
11. Ibid., 47.
12. See for example Edward Farley, *Faith and Beauty*, viii.

messianism or ecological Darwinism or nihilistic despair, it may evoke responses of confession (speaking the truth about our alienated and alienating ways-of-being), repentance (embodying new possibilities), lamentation (breaking through numbness and empowering action by grieving what has been lost), and, finally, hope (because the divine creativity that both tears down and builds up is still efficacious even in the midst of loss).

No doubt divine judgment is a perilous category. It may well be that its destructive potential outweighs its redemptive possibilities. Too easily the pious imagination attributes suffering to divine judgment—"what have I done to deserve this?" Beyond personal piety, most public declarations of divine judgment of recent memory have been massively misguided, whether proclaiming 9/11 as divine judgment for the wickedness of pagans, abortionists, feminists, gays, lesbians, and the ACLU (as Jerry Falwell pronounced) or Hurricane Katrina as judgment on the sin-loving city of New Orleans (with apologies to the coasts of Alabama and Mississippi which apparently constitute divine collateral damage).

I do not wish to moralize suffering, as if all suffering could be located within a coherent moral order. That vision is neither biblical nor moral. But does this mean that it cannot be potentially redemptive to use the category of divine judgment to name the suffering born of destructive ways-of-being? Likewise, I do not wish to justify invocations of "divine judgment" that are in reality thinly veiled ideological power plays. But does this mean it cannot ever be potentially redemptive to use the category of divine judgment to name socioeconomic and political-ideological ways-of-being that do violence to creation and thus sow the seeds of destruction?

I believe that judgment—*in some sense*[13]—can be a crucial aspect of the divine activity. In my effort to sort out what "in some sense" means, I am influenced again by H. Richard Niebuhr. Reflecting on God's activity in the context of World War II, Niebuhr writes:

> God is always in history; [God] is the structure of things, the source of all meaning, the "I am that I am," that which is that it is; the rock against which we beat in vain.... That structure of the universe, that creative will, can no more be said to interfere brutally in history than the violated laws of my organism can be said to interfere brutally with my life if they make me pay the cost of my violation. That structure of the universe, that will of God, does bring war and depression upon us when we bring it upon

---

13. I am reminded of a comment overheard by James Gustafson: when theologians say "in some sense" they usually cannot say in *what* sense.

ourselves, for we live in the kind of world which visits our iniquities upon us and our children, no matter how much we pray and desire that it be otherwise.[14]

Here God is the "structure of things" or the "structure of the universe," and judgment names the apparently inevitable consequences of violating that structure. Niebuhr's organic analogy makes this clear: it does not require special divine agency to account for, say, a headache after drinking too much wine. Fearful and rapacious self-assertion leads to conflict. Pumping CO_2 into the atmosphere traps radiant heat and warms the planet. Our iniquities are visited upon our children, "no matter how much we pray and desire that it be otherwise."

However, if these "judgments" can be accounted for exhaustively through biological or social or chemical causality, what sense does it make to speak of *God* at all? Is it not better simply to speak of the natural consequences of our behavior? Of course a theocentric piety does not make detached, rational calculations as to how best to construe the world; it has been shaped by communal practice to *see* the activity of God in all things. Nevertheless, given the way the affirmation of divine agency creates tensions around questions of scientific causality, human freedom and responsibility, evil and suffering, and so on, the question of how divine judgment does or does not intersect with natural causality is not without merit.

Perhaps Niebuhr's "two-aspect theory of history" provides a helpful conceptuality for addressing these issues.[15] Niebuhr distinguishes between "external history" and "internal history." External history is history measured by cause and effect (I-it in Martin Buber's terms), perceivable to the senses and explainable in terms of biological or sociological or chemical functions and forces. Internal history is history open to ethical values, spiritual meanings, and personal encounters (I-thou in Buber's terms). Internal history is also the locus of revelation. For Niebuhr, external history and internal history constitute a "duality in union," distinction without separation.

Thus the same historical moment—in this case, the ecological crisis—may be read in two ways. It may be read "externally" as a concatenation of chemical and physical and political and economic functions and forces. It also may be read "internally" (by an interpreter shaped by a particular

---

14. Niebuhr, "The Only Way Into the Kingdom," 15.
15. Niebuhr, *Meaning of Revelation*, 43–90.

communal tradition) as divine judgment and redemption, inviting fitting and faithful response.

Of course many questions linger. As with the biblical text itself, so here: judgment appears to fall indiscriminately, and it is precisely the most vulnerable ones (and certainly in the case of ecological disaster, the most innocent ones) who suffer the first and heaviest blows. Perhaps this grim reality is not the fruit of judgment but rather that which is being judged: a system so rigged that the polluters prosper while the rising seas wash over the innocent. To the pious imagination, the construal of divine judgment does not provide satisfactory answers to these questions. But it does evoke confession and lamentation, that such is the world and such have we made it.

In any case, I think it is crucial to affirm, following Abraham Heschel, that divine wrath is an element of divine pathos, that anger is an "interlude" in the larger tale of divine love.[16] Or, to retrieve the dialectic of judgment and redemption, it is crucial to affirm that the purpose of judgment is redemption, or better, that in God's judging is God's redeeming. The divine creative process both judges and redeems, destructs and constructs, but it is *one* process: God the Creator, Judge, and Redeemer. And as the cross reminds us, even judgment is a mode of divine presence, not absence. No matter how deeply we wound or are wounded, the judging-redeeming love of God runs deeper still. Even in judgment, even in wrath, divine creativity is at work. Fructifying grace flows even in the midst of calamity.

Hope in Redeemed Selves

However, the question remains: What self can bear this fructifying grace into a world that is marred by violence? What self can be an agent (and not merely a patient) in this ongoing judging and redeeming work? What self can respond to beauty? What self can be beautiful? What self can hope? Providing comprehensive answers to these questions would require a fully formed theological anthropology, which is well beyond the scope of this project. But it is necessary to say a word about the structure of the self that may truncate or obliterate hope, and then the self in a state of redemption that makes hope possible. I propose drawing on a montage of sources (in an admittedly cursory way), especially evolutionary biology and process categories, to sketch out the contours of the self that hopes.

---

16. See Heschel, *Prophets*, vol. 1, 59–78.

Philip Hefner is professor emeritus of systematic theology at the Lutheran School of Theology in Chicago, and his work focuses on the interaction of religion and science. Especially important for my purposes is his attempt to develop a "bio-cultural" understanding of the human being. In *The Human Factor*, Hefner interprets human beings as thoroughly natural creatures, emergents from evolutionary processes. He describes human beings as two-natured creatures, the synthesis of two lines of code: genetic and cultural. We are the products of evolution and culture. We are also the producers of culture, and through culture, the shapers of evolution as well. As Hefner puts it in theological terms, we are not only created, we are also co-creators.[17]

For Hefner, the emergence of human freedom is an expression of God's intention for creation. Through the evolutionary process a creature has emerged who represents the possibilities for freedom inherent in creation and who points to the purpose of creation. The human being thus stands at the intersection of genes and culture, nature and spirit. As created, the human being is fully embedded in and a product of natural processes. Thus it can be said that nature participates in human beings as much as human beings participate in nature. As co-creator, however, the human being is capable of transcending natural processes, moving in a "zone of freedom" that allows it to transcend and thus work for the wholeness of creation in response to the divine call.[18]

However, as the product of two lines of code, as the gradual emergence of spirit/culture out of nature/genes, there will be inevitable struggles and tensions along the way. The created co-creator does not emerge with a divine fiat. It emerges through natural processes over billions of years. Thus only gradually will the created co-creator grow to its full destiny. There is a natural and inevitable gap between created creature and co-creative creature, and it is in this gap that concupiscence and idolatry and countless other self-securing strategies take root.

We see similar dynamics at work in Marjorie Hewitt Suchocki's process influenced theological anthropology. In *Fall to Violence*, Suchocki sees sin as rooted in innate human aggressiveness and violence. As we saw with Hefner, human beings are the confluence of genetic and cultural coding. The genetic coding includes our reptilian brains, calibrated as they are for hyper-attentiveness to self-preservation and propagation. We cannot leave

---

17. Hefner, *Human Factor*, 35–39.
18. Ibid., 42.

our reptilian brains behind. This innate propensity for violence is exacerbated by solidarity among human beings that causes us to share one another's pain and thus increases the threatened nature of our vulnerability, and it is institutionalized and passed on through social structures. However, God's continuing creative call is toward the transcendence of unnecessary violence and the turning of our aggressiveness from destructive to creative ends.

This overcoming of sin is rooted in the creative activity of God, interpreted in the categories of process theology. Every actual occasion is a process of receiving the past, creatively becoming in the present, and projecting into the future, that is, memory, empathy, and imagination.[19] As Whitehead famously said, God is not an exception to this metaphysical structure but is rather its chief exemplification. So the divine memory is truth: the absolute knowledge of what every entity has become. The divine empathy is love: the absolute acceptance of every entity as it has become in the divine life and in the life of the world. And the divine imagination is beauty: the integration of every entity into the highest possible divine harmony. This is the divine foundation of forgiveness, for forgiveness itself is rooted in memory of the violation, empathy toward the well-being of the victim and the violator, and imagination toward a reconciled future. Only such forgiveness makes possible the well-being of creation. Only such forgiveness makes possible hope.

Both Hefner and Suchocki root the self and its propensity for destructiveness in biology and evolution. Suchocki draws on process categories to begin mapping out the contours of a self that has been set free from this congenital propensity to violence. Catherine Keller also draws on process categories in her analysis of the self, in addition to a diverse range of other resources. In *From a Broken Web*, Keller explores what she calls separative, soluble, and influent selves. Western modes of selfhood, she argues, have been decisively and destructively shaped by the myth of separation, that is, that a subject is what it is by virtue of its separation from everything else. The separative self fears attachments and relationality as potential diminutions of its invulnerable selfhood. Keller associates this separative self with Descartes's doubt-filled *cogito* and its attendant metaphysical dualism.[20] The separative self thus creates its mirror opposite, the soluble self, which conforms to and dissolves within the separative self's presence. These modes of selfhood have been gendered historically, and have led to

---

19. Suchocki, *Fall to Violence*, chapter 9.
20. Keller, *From a Broken Web*, 11.

the hypermasculine, seemingly inviolable male self that is actually beset by terrors and doubt and so must constantly, violently establish itself over against the other; and the self-dispersing female self that is ever under threat of conforming to the male/separative self or dissolving altogether.

Keller imagines a third mode of selfhood, an influent or connective self, and here she draws on process themes. She begins with an apologia for metaphysics: we are all inevitably metaphysical, she says. Metaphysics is "nothing but the description of the generalities which apply to all the details of practice."[21] True, feminists cannot be metaphysical in a disembodied or totalizing way. Multiplicity and particularity must not be squeezed into the Procrustean bed of a metaphysical system. But we all have a way of seeing (*theoria*)—or failing to see—the connections between things.

Having argued for a place for (process) metaphysics, Keller takes our selves on a journey through Western intellectual history. For Aristotle, she argues, the self is a substance which by definition cannot be *in* another thing. Augustine makes this impermeable self the individual's soul. Keller notes that Augustine demonstrates some "mystical memory" of non-separative oceanic feelings, but because he fears particularity, he wants to flee from the many to the one.[22] As she says elsewhere in reference to Augustine, "the autobiographical Christian self excels in its capacity to transcend its bodily, social and ecological contexts."[23] This sets the Christian theological tradition on its trajectory toward God as the Absolutely Other, mirroring the impermeable substantial soul, drained of all mutuality, reciprocity, and vulnerability. Trinitarian trajectories posited relationality as essential to the divine, but the insistence on the simplicity and changelessness of God vitiated any real relations between the triune God and creation (and within the triune God itself). Thus we have a separative (male) self/soul mirroring a separative (male) God.

There are other strands in Western intellectual history, found in David Hume (who critiques the substantial self and locates the self, ambiguously, in perception), William James (the self as a "stream of consciousness"), and Martin Buber (the self/I coming to be only in relation to the other/Thou). These strands are woven together in Whitehead's process thought. For Whitehead, reality is made up, not of things or substances, but of events: actual occasions (or actual entities). Actual occasions "feel" (prehend) the

---

21. Ibid., 157 (quoting Whitehead).
22. Ibid., 165. Keller develops this theme further in *Face of the Deep*, chapter 4.
23. Keller, *Face of the Deep*, 68.

whole causal nexus, exercise freedom and creativity within the present to actualize particular possibilities (concrescence), and then pass out of existence (and thus are prehended by future actual occasions).

Keller finds this metaphysic useful in several ways. It suggests universal permeability: "every actual entity is present in every other actual entity."[24] It also suggests universal fluidity and flux: every actual occasion comes to be, achieves satisfaction, passes away, and then is prehended anew. It imagines the self, not as a fixed substance, but as an event, a process. The self is made over and over again in the creative fusing of the prehended past with future possibilities. In this sense, there is not one self but many selves. This self (or these selves) is (are) differentiated, not by cutting off all relations and clinging to simplicity, but through width of relationality and depth of complexity.

As we wade through Keller's linguistic legerdemain we can trace the contours of her process, connective, influent, liquid, concrescing-and-dissolving self. As with Hefner and Suchocki, Keller's process self is embedded in nature. It emerges out of nature. Causality is bottom-up, not top-down. True, we might say the divine "lures" the self into existence, but ultimately it is evolutionary processes that generate a nervous system capable of organizing otherwise disparate actual occasions into a center of experience. And this self, its constituent actual occasions, the whole process by which it comes into being—these are not unique to human selves. Whitehead imagined positing something like a soul in any living thing that had an organizing center of experience. But even beyond that, experience itself goes "all the way down" for Whitehead. All actual occasions prehend ("feel") and respond to all other actual occasions. There is no ontological dividing line between human selves/souls and the rest of nature.

Thus in the process vision, all of reality is a communion of subjects rather than a collection of objects (to paraphrase Thomas Berry). Or, as Keller puts it, "Human becoming looks cramped and cancerous—unless we collude more wisely with the elements, the plants, the beasts, and each other."[25] Affirming the embeddedness of the self in nature invites us to see (proto-)selves in nature, and this has profound ethical implications. To quote Keller again: "The relation to the face, always most intensely focused in the interhuman, now demands of us planetary practices which find 'face'

---

24. Ibid., 184 (quoting Whitehead).
25. Ibid., 140.

across the width of the world."[26] Levinas might have resisted such an expansive understanding of the face, fearing its use as an evasion of the interhuman, but Keller's process vision propels her to extend the infinite ethical demands of the face to all of nature.

Keller's vision also allows us to affirm the *incommunicabilis*, the irreducibility, the nontransferable uniqueness of selves without succumbing to a destructive dualism as did Philip Rolnick in our discussion in Chapter 4. We see this perhaps most clearly in her "being private/being public" ontological dyad.[27] There is a potential danger in Keller's vision, in that the fluid self risks becoming the soluble self. Given that all other actual occasions flow into it and it ultimately flows into all other actual occasions, the process self is radically public, radically communitarian—and radically at risk of losing all boundaries and "sliding into a soft undifferentiated slime of emotional dependencies."[28] However, in the present moment of self-creation, the self is not and cannot be prehended by any other actual occasion. As Whitehead puts it, "the vast causal independence of contemporary occasions is the preservative elbow-room within the universe."[29] This "elbowroom" is precisely the freedom of the self to be who it is and to self-create. It is the irreducible still point, the nontransferable isness, the *incommunicabilis* of the self that cannot be engulfed by the rest of universe or the separative self, not to mention the totalitarian fantasies of economic or scientific "advancement."

Each of these visions of anthropology and selfhood, created co-creator, human beings as expressive of and caught up in memory, empathy, and imagination, and Keller's influent selves offers important insights into the human predicament and what may make for human freedom. But what is missing is a deeper thematization of the theological contours of the human need for redemption.

It is the deepest human need to be founded, to be secured against the radical contingencies and uncertainties of existence.[30] Lacking such founding, human beings lash about in idolatry, trying to fill an infinite horizon with finite goods. This is Tillich's concupiscence, the infinite desire to cram the world into one's mouth. This is Hefner's creative co-creator, only

---

26. Ibid., 7.
27. Keller, *From a Broken Web*, 228–33.
28. Ibid., 2.
29. Whitehead, *Adventures of Ideas*, 195.
30. On "founding" see Edward Farley, *Divine Empathy*, chapter 5.

inhabiting its "zone of freedom" in bondage to its genetic coding. This is Suchocki's reptilian self, driven to violence because of truncated memory, empathy, and imagination. This is Keller's separative self, seeking to secure itself, to establish itself, by reducing all else to others and then consuming them. Needless to say, this disordered devouring of the finite world has devastating ecological implications. The substantial/separative self in search of ultimate security may be the greatest threat to planetary well-being.

Of course Keller's fluid self hardly offers a solid founding. Indeed, it is an anti-founding, a liquid flow, a creative chaotic becoming. "To love is to bear with the chaos."[31] And so the question of redemption again: Is it possible to be a liquid self at peace with its chaotic fluidity? Is it possible to relinquish the grip of idolatry, to find ontological courage, "a willingness to accept the relativity and particularity of all finite goods, a consent to finitude as tragic, and a willingness to risk one's actual being in decision and creativity" in the midst of the flux and the flow?[32]

The testimony of the Christian tradition (and not the Christian tradition alone) is that, yes, the (fluid) self can exist amidst the ebbs and flows and chaotic cascades of existence without clinging idolatrously to finite things for security. But such a self must be founded in God—and not a god who/which is another finite thing, even the greatest finite thing, which would simply be another idol that would fail to found. And so we find ourselves back with Calvin, unable to speak of self-and-world without also speaking of God. Whether and how Keller's "tehomic deity"[33] or Whitehead's "great companion—the fellow-sufferer who understands"[34] or Farley's "Redeemer, Creativity, and Holy One"[35] or some other construal of the divine answers to the need for a non-idolatrous founding, it seems clear that creative dwelling in and with nature is not simply a matter of more comprehensive science or sharper ethical exhortation or even imagining a self embedded in nature and yet possessed of unique ethical meaning and responsibilities. It is, rather, a matter of redemption: freedom from the effects of idolatry.[36]

In the previous chapter we explored the tragic structure of the cosmic process. Edward Farley sees this tragic structure as the most fundamental

31. Keller, *Face of the Deep*, 29.
32. Farley, *Divine Empathy*, 67.
33. Keller, *Face of the Deep*, chapter 13.
34. Whitehead, *Process and Reality*, 351.
35. Farley, *Divine Empathy*, 144.
36. Ibid., 67.

feature of the human condition.[37] In an evolutionary world, conditions of well-being are interconnected with conditions of suffering. Existence is not tragic simply because it is inevitably full of suffering. It is tragic because the very goods of existence—creativity, beauty, love—entail suffering.

For Farley, this is the root of evil. Contrary to the Augustinian tradition which interprets sin as the *root* of suffering, the tragic paradigm interprets sin as the *result* of suffering. The vulnerable and tragically structured human condition is the occasion for the corruption of human freedom. It does not cause such a corruption. It is possible to live with courage and compassion in the midst of vulnerability and suffering. But the human animal's need to secure itself in the midst of such vulnerability is virtually overwhelming. So we cling to various goods at hand, finite realities, to provide for us the security we seek. We give them absolute loyalty and violently defend them against any threats. When they fail us, as they inevitably do, we despise them and thrash about in despair. This idolatry prevents us from loving the things of this world as they are, in their fragile beauty. By insisting they secure us, we distort them and ourselves.

The possibility of living with courage and compassion despite our vulnerability in the midst of a tragically structured cosmic process is grounded in God. In being founded in God, we are set free from our idolatry. We are free to enjoy the beauty of the finite world without insisting that it fulfill our infinite horizon of desire. We can consent in humility to the tragic structure of the cosmic process, the conflicts and struggles and sufferings which are the inevitable concomitants of possibilities for growth and creativity and beauty. Yet more than consent: we are free to risk our being in living with creativity and compassion with and for our fellow suffering creatures.

It is this redeemed self that can hope. It this self that can be an agent (and not merely a patient) in the ongoing judging and redeeming work of God. It is this self can respond to beauty.

Firing the Loving Answer: Hope in Beauty

"For what is Beauty, if it doth not fire the loving answer of an eager soul?"

—Robert Bridges

---

37. See Farley, *Good and Evil*.

In *Ecologies of the Heart,* E. N. Anderson argues that ecological problems are due to human choice, and human choice is passionate. Thus only a full engagement of the human passionate life can counteract the natural human propensity to value even a very small present good over a very large future good. What is needed, in other words, is an ecological ethic "of the heart." "Why is it so hard," conservation biologist David Orr writes, "to talk about love, the most powerful of human emotions, in relation to science, the most powerful and far-reaching of human activities?"[38] Anderson himself advocates for a kind of post-traditional ecological religiosity, one that establishes a "moral code by embedding it in emotionally compelling communal systems of symbols, beliefs, and ceremonies."[39] He acknowledges that most existing religions are deeply problematic in terms of their ecological coding, and that it would be very difficult if not impossible to simply dust off an ancient animistic world view and try to adopt it in a postmodern scientific context. However, "this does not stop us from invoking an aesthetic and moral system that allows us to care."[40] In a similar way, John Gatta writes:

> Amending this error [the tragic error of the voracious consumption of the earth] will require a change of heart, a drastic renewal of reverence such as Albert Schweitzer had only begun to imagine. Environmental reverence, like any other virtue, must be instilled through deliberate training and exercise. *First of all, though, the virtue's beauty must be imagined and articulated persuasively enough to seem appealing.*[41]

How do we make the virtue of "environmental reverence" beautiful? What place might beauty have in construing a hopeful trajectory in the context of ecological diminishment? How might beauty "fire the loving answer of an eager soul"?

Some would consider it passé, naïve, even dangerous to raise the question of beauty in our context. Postmodernism has thoroughly exposed and dismantled beauty as one more tantalizing yet totalizing metanarrative from which we must be liberated. Postmodern art celebrates precisely this freedom from classical canons of beauty, harmony, form, and so on. Of course the eclipse of beauty began much earlier in the Western religious and philosophical tradition. In its contestation with a "paganism"

---

38. Quoted in Anderson, *Ecologies of the Heart,* 5.
39. Ibid., 162.
40. Ibid., 173.
41. Gatta, *Making Nature Sacred,* 243 (my emphasis).

that viewed nature as a manifestation of sacred power, early Hebrew religion was marked by a deep ambivalence toward natural beauty. Protestant Christianity shared and even intensified this suspicion. Over against Roman Catholic aestheticism, natural theology, and alleged syncretism, Protestant Christianity adopted an iconoclasm, a logocentric stringency, and a kind of moral asceticism that repudiated the presence of sacred power in nature and rejected the softening lure of the aesthetic life.

This sketch oversimplifies complex matters, to be sure, but it points to a suspicion—or better, a hunch—that the eclipse of beauty and the eclipse of nature are interconnected. Human beings who have not been formed in the practice of creating and responding to beauty will be ill-equipped to dwell with and in nature: so goes my hunch. Thus the recovery of a robust sensibility to beauty in all its joy and pathos may very well feed a robust and hope-filled ecological praxis.

Of course beauty has played a significant role in the modern ecological movement. The aesthetic response to pleasing landscapes, charismatic animals, and so on, has long been used to motivate conservationist efforts. Recall David Brower's use of photography to mobilize public opposition to the Echo Park Dam in Utah's Dinosaur National Monument and his relation with Ansel Adams and an emerging natural photography movement. Many of the early pioneers of environmental activism were deeply imprinted by embodied aesthetic experiences in nature, and art forms such as landscape painting, nature photography, and nature writing evolved concurrently with the environmental movement.[42] Nevertheless, beauty has not figured prominently in reflections on ecological ethics, and its place in an ecological theology is likewise ambiguous.

Edward Farley has traced four prominent interpretations in the Western story of beauty: what he calls the "great theory of beauty," beauty as proportion or harmony (seen from Hellenic times to the eighteenth century); beauty as sensibility, that is, as subjective response to objective stimuli (the "turn to the subject" in the eighteenth century); beauty as "consenting benevolence" drawn from the theological aesthetics of Jonathan Edwards; and beauty as self-transcending and transcendental dimension of experience in Kant and Schopenhauer.[43]

---

42. See for example Hargrove, *Foundations of Environmental Ethics*, chapters 3 and 4, and Gatta, *Making Nature Sacred*.

43. Farley, *Faith and Beauty*, 118.

Several insights drawn from this complex constellation of traditions might prove helpful for my attempt to ground hope in beauty. First, because nothing can exist without having some form, some proportion or harmony of contrasts, every existing entity has some measure of beauty. To be is to be beautiful.[44] Second, because beauty is harmony emerging out of chaos, chaos ever lurks at its edges, clings to it as a shadow of sorts—indeed, the chaotic contrast is part of what constitutes beauty.[45] This means that beauty is necessarily fragile, always subject to disintegration. It also means that beauty has an element of pathos: it is always passing, always only a momentary harmonization of contrasts in the midst of swirling process and chaos.[46] Third, the subjective experience of beauty is complex. Certainly pleasure is a part of this experience, but because beauty contains an element of pathos, the experience of beauty also has an element of the pathetic (sympathy, sorrow). Further, the experience of beauty as the "sublime" carries with it the sense of awe and even fear or dread, something akin to Rudolph Otto's *mysterium tremendum et fascinans*.[47] These three themes—beauty as being, beauty as pathos, and beauty as an experience of pleasure, pathos, and the sublime—deepen and complexify our understanding of beauty and will prove helpful in exploring the connection between beauty and hope.

Holmes Rolston picks up many of these aesthetic themes in his *Environmental Ethics*. Among the many values he finds carried in nature is the aesthetic: "the disappearance of any species represents a great aesthetic loss for the entire world," as he quotes A. F. Coimbra-Filho.[48] We have seen this before, of course. Leopold's land ethic also had an aesthetic component: "a thing is right when it tends to preserve the integrity, stability and beauty of the biotic community."[49] It is also a dominant motif in theological reflection on creation, as I noted above in the discussion of the goodness (utilitarian, intrinsic, aesthetic, and doxological) of the cosmic process.

Both Leopold and Rolston argue that beauty is not merely a subjective response of pleasure to external stimuli but is in some sense present or "carried in" (Rolston's term) nature. Rolston states that nature has aesthetic power, that is, the power to produce aesthetic properties, even if it is not

---

44. Ibid., 17.
45. Ibid., 19.
46. Ibid., 101–3.
47. Ibid., 36–38.
48. Rolston, *Environmental Ethics*, 10.
49. Leopold, *Sand County Almanac*, 262.

until the human animal (also a product of nature) arrives that the capacity for aesthetic experience fully emerges. As he says, "nature carries aesthetic properties objectively, and these are ignited in the subjective experience of the arriving beholder."[50] And, though aesthetic sensibility may emerge most fully in the human animal, this does not mean that we can properly deny any kind of aesthetic sensibility to nonhuman animals: "Unless we think that birds and beasts have no experience at all, it is difficult to deny them the precursors of aesthetic experience."[51]

So, then, beauty is both an objective aspect of existing entities and also a subjective response to those existing entities (insofar as object-subject language is even meaningful in this context). To be is to possess some measure of beauty, to be some fit of form and function, some harmony of contrasts, though beauty, like being itself, is ever fragile and subject to disintegration. Human animals, and arguably many other animals, are sensible to beauty, responsive to beauty, whether experienced as pleasurable, as pathetic, or as the sublime.

Beauty is not mere prettiness, that which is pleasing to the human eye. Beauty includes elements of pathos, fragility, vulnerability, suffering, death. Chaos clings to order. Chaos is both the possibility of ever-emerging novelty and creativity, and the possibility of disintegration and dissolution. If our understanding of beauty cannot include pathos, cannot absorb these negativities, then it will ever serve as a censure of nature[52] and will compel us to "prettify" it—that is, to humanize and thus to destroy nature as nature. But an understanding of beauty that includes pathos can respond to (even consent to) the fragile, chaotic, ever dying-and-living nature we actually participate in. As Rolston says: "Great beauty, like great music, is often in a minor key."[53] Or to quote Leopold: "One of the penalties of an ecological education is one lives in a world of wounds."[54]

Not only must our understanding of beauty be deepened with this awareness of pathos, but it also must be broadened with concepts of space and time and scale that are appropriate to the cosmic process. "Environmental

---

50. Ibid., 235.

51. Ibid., 234. This is a prominent theme in process thought as well. See for example Charles Hartshorne's discussion of the aesthetic dimension of bird song *for the bird* in *Born to Sing*.

52. See for example Sideris, "Writing Straight with Crooked Lines."

53. Rolston, *Environmental Ethics*, 245.

54. Leopold, *Round River*, 165.

ethics," Rolston argues, "stretches us out from our individualistic, self-centered perspectives into a consideration of *systemic* beauty."[55] This shift in perception from the individual to the systemic is also a major emphasis in the various dark green ecological ethics I mentioned earlier. Whether the land ethic or Gaia theory or deep ecology or ecofeminism, each in its own way challenges regnant hegemonic individualistic modes of thought and encourages human animals to "think like a mountain," to shift perspectives to scales appropriate to natural systems. In this way, the seeming ugliness of individual moments—the lion tearing at the flesh of the gazelle, the rotting carcass of the deer—are seen in the larger context of the thriving biotic system, and are in fact essential elements of the system's capacity to generate beauty.[56] "Nature's beauty can be costly and tragic, yet nature is a scene of beauty ever reasserting itself in the face of destruction."[57]

I have argued that a sufficiently robust understanding of beauty—beauty as containing elements of pathos, beauty as systemic—can serve as a motivation for "environmental reverence" and thus as a cause for hope in the context of ecological diminishment. Rather than relying solely on enlightened self-interest, individualistic anthropocentrism, or various intellectual analyses of sociopolitical, gendered, and economic structures (important as these are), we may appeal to beauty: the intrinsic beauty of being itself, beauty as fit of form and function, as harmony of contrasts, at both the individual and the systemic level, ever surging forward in the midst of chaos and pathos, "firing the loving answer of an eager soul." The human animal responds to such beauty both as pleasing and also as pathetic, and thus it will be necessary to cultivate practices which form human animals in a sensibility to beauty that transcends the banality of prettiness.

For Jonathan Edwards, the beauty of nature is gloriously real, but it is secondary beauty. Primary beauty is "consent, propensity and union of heart to being in general, which is immediately exercised in general good will."[58] What is most beautiful for Edwards is the beauty of compassion, the beauty of the self flowing out in consent to and love for all being. In a

---

55. Ibid., 241 (my emphasis).

56. This approach has a long history in Christian theodicy: the beauty of the whole is enhanced by the shadows of darkness and suffering. This is not a central question for this project, so we need not tarry here, but suffice it to say that I think the systemic aesthetic approach may be valuable in the context of "amoral" nature, but once moral culpability enters the system (in human animals), the aesthetic as a theodicy becomes problematic.

57. Rolston, *Environmental Ethics*, 241.

58. Edwards, *Nature of True Virtue*, 3.

similar way, Schopenhauer argues that it is beauty that summons human beings out of their self-preoccupation and willing, that is, beauty evokes self-transcendence.[59] For Edwards, of course, in this way human beings (and all other creatures) mirror the outflowing, self-giving love of the Trinity. The beauty of the self is precisely its *imago Dei*, its self-emptying, its self-transcending, its outflowing in consent to and love for all being. To be is to be beautiful, and to respond to beauty in compassionate self-transcendence is likewise to be beautiful.

From a process perspective we may affirm that God, too, is open to the beauty of the cosmic process, not simply creative of but responsive to its pleasure and its pathos. God does not call the worlds into being *ex nihilo* but rather was and is and always will be luring forth from the *tehom*—the ocean, the deep, the abyss—fecund possibilities and integrating the resulting actualities into the highest possible harmony. Our hope lies not only in the fragile beauty of the cosmic process itself, which summons forth a loving response, nor solely in the beauty of the redeemed influent overflowing self making such a response, but also in the divine creativity (even the divine humility) that lures forth from this graced and grieving cosmic process ever new manifestations of beauty. There is hope because all creation is and can be beautiful, not by divine fiat, but by divine allurement.

And so we have returned to Calvin and to the "many bonds" that join God, self, and world. Perhaps most essential of these bonds is the bond of beauty itself, and it is here, in beauty weaving together God, self, and world, that our hope is finally to be found. It is found in the fragile beauty of every creature, evoking wonder and compassion, firing the loving answer of an eager soul, luring the self out of its solipsism. It is found in that eager soul itself, in the beauty of a redeemed self, set free from idolatrous self-securing to go out to meet the other in love. And it is found in the beauty of the divine creativity that lures forth ever-new, fecund possibilities and the divine love that gathers up all the beautiful and broken creatures into the deepest possible harmony.

Our hope was only ever in the efficacy of Beauty.

---

59. See Farley, *Faith and Beauty*, 59–62.

6

Practicing the New Creation

Julian of Norwich, one of the great mystics of the fourteenth century, had a vision of creation as

> something small, no bigger than a hazelnut, lying in the palm of my hand, and I perceived that it was round as any ball. I looked at it and thought: What can this be? And I was given this general answer: It is everything which is made. I was amazed that it could last, for I thought that it was so little that it could suddenly fall into nothing. And I was answered in my understanding: It lasts and always will, because God loves it; and thus everything has being through the love of God.[1]

The hazelnut is a sign of hope, a sign that divine love can and will sustain even so small and fragile a creation, suspended as it is over nothingness. Julian envisions God as the great creator and lover and protector of creation, and throughout *Showings* she repeats the refrain: "all will be well, and every kind of thing will be well."[2] This is perhaps the most elemental and urgent of Christian affirmations.

In a similar way, philosopher Erazim Kohak writes that it is the knowledge that "it will be—or perhaps eternally is—*all right*" that makes bearable "the intense, anguished beauty of children playing in the sun by the river, heedless of the horizon about to close in upon them."[3] With greenhouse gases and temperatures increasing, with rising sea levels and acidifying oceans, with the loss of species and whole ecosystems, with deteriorating

---

1. Julian of Norwich, *Showings*, 130.
2. Ibid., 149.
3. Kohak, *Embers and the Stars*, 162.

food chains and diminishing reserves of fresh water, with destructive and unpredictable weather, with loss of coastlines and arable land leading to ever-greater migrations and inevitable violent conflicts—indeed the horizon is closing in upon our children and their children. We live in a time of climate chaos and ecological diminishment. It may be that only this primal hope, hope that "all will be well," can enable us to live with courage, creativity, and compassion in the midst of such loss.

But what contemporary shape does such an elemental hope take? We need a hope that can sustain equanimity (or what Schleiermacher calls "blessedness") in the midst of distress, enabling us to respond to the unfolding diminishment of our world with wisdom and compassion rather than fear and violence. We also need a hope that can foster engaged praxis on behalf of a suffering creation. We need a hope that both settles and unsettles, comforts and afflicts, plants and plucks up. And if it is to be a hope for *this* creation (and not some other), it must be a hope that enfolds the cosmic process, in all its beauty and brokenness, rather than leaves it behind. It must be a humble hope, remaining resolutely grounded in the dirt.

I have argued that Jürgen Moltmann and Sallie McFague endeavor to name such a hope in the midst of ecological diminishment, but ultimately fall short. Moltmann walks the fault line between a hopeful orientation toward the future and a humble cherishing of the good, green earth. However, despite his passionate and commendable efforts to preserve the many beautiful and broken creatures of the earth, they are ultimately swallowed up—redeemed, yes, but denatured—by an eschatological vision that cannot finally give space to the tragic, the wild, the other-than-human. In the end, Moltmann's hope cannot remain grounded in the dirt.

McFague, too, walks the fault line between hope and humility, but despite her sometimes passionate rhetoric, her hope is finally curtailed by the bondage of the human will. If indeed the divine creativity at work in the world is finally restrained by human consent, given the vulnerability and the tragic structure of the human condition, given the resulting idolatry and concupiscence, a more vital understanding of the possibility of human redemption is needed in order to make hope a robust possibility. In the end, the subjunctive dimension of McFague's vision thins its hopefulness to the point of transparency.

I have argued for a hope that is humble, grounded in the dirt, a hope that stands in solidarity with the entire cosmic process in which we are embedded, a cosmic process that is good and graced but also tragically structured and not always amenable to human strivings. It is this creation, and not some other, to which a humble hope consents.

I have also argued for a humility that is hopeful, that is, grounded not only in the cosmic process but also in the redemptive possibilities of the divine creativity at work in all things. The three theological foci (God, self, and world) find their humble and hopeful orientation as they are woven together with beauty: the beauty of the other that summons the self out of its solipsism, the beauty of the self coming out to meet the other, and the beauty of divine creativity that lures forth ever-new, fecund possibilities and divine love that gathers up all the beautiful and broken actualities into the deepest possible harmony. Hope for the world is hope in Beauty.

Of course these reflections represent only faltering steps; many questions remain unanswered. Perhaps most urgent is the question of how such a hope enables passionate praxis on behalf of a suffering creation. History is replete with constructions of hope that eviscerate rather than enable such praxis. What might a humble and hopeful praxis look like?

Pace Richard Dawkins, Sam Harris, and Daniel Dennett (the "New Atheists"), I believe it is a religious world view, rather than a secular-scientific one, which offers the greatest hope for a humane way-of-being-in-the-world in the midst of ecological diminishment. My work focuses on the Christian tradition as a religious response because, first, it is what I know, and, second, it is a dominant voice in my North American context. But I am confident there are community-forming, compassion-forming patterns and processes at work in other religious traditions, and in this we are companions on the road.

In articulating his understanding of eschatology, Calvin had little patience for speculative fantasy. He dismissed what he considered superfluous questions, but in the process of dismissing them, he often provided the seeds of an answer. One such superfluous question was this: why will there be a new creation, a new earth? We know (so the thinking went) that the old creation was ordered to human ends, that is, to provide food for human beings. If we will not have to eat in the new creation, then we will no longer need the earth to provide for our needs. Why, then, a new creation?

Calvin's response is illuminating. He says that in the "very sight of [the new creation] there will be such pleasantness, such sweetness in the knowledge of it alone, without the use of it, that this happiness will far surpass all the amenities that we now enjoy."[4] Thus the contemplation of creation in the eschaton will be sublime beyond anything we have heretofore experienced because we will be able to contemplate it apart from our need of it. That is, we will be able to contemplate the beauty of creation without regard to its utility, to enjoy its goodness in itself, not merely its goodness for us. Perhaps a humble and hopeful praxis can take this form of "practicing the new creation."

One acute challenge facing the Christian community in its effort to "practice the new creation" is the impoverishment of its worship. Thomas Berry reflects on the depletion of imagination and language as a result of ecological diminishment:

> We should be clear about what happens when we destroy the living forms of this planet. The first consequence is that we destroy modes of divine presence. If we have a wonderful sense of the divine, it is because we live amid such awesome magnificence.... If we lived on the moon, our mind and emotions, our speech, our imagination, our sense of the divine would all reflect the desolation of the lunar landscape.[5]

Paul Ricoeur has argued that prophetic proclamation (the Word) exists in creative tension with sacred manifestation in nature.[6] Though there has been a strong trajectory in both the biblical theology movement and the Barthian hermeneutic of much postliberal theology to read prophetic proclamation as the negation of sacred manifestation, Ricoeur maintains that manifestation is the ground of meaning for proclamation. If this is so, then ecological diminishment creates a crisis of language: cut off from sacred manifestation in nature that gives meaning to our words, our proclamation becomes incoherent.[7] In a similar way, Paul Tillich argues that the celebration of the sacraments depends for its efficacy in part on the power of nature to bear sacramental power: "If nature loses its power, the sacrament becomes arbitrary and insignificant."[8] If the intrinsic power of grain

---

4. Calvin, *Institutes*, 1006-7.
5. Berry, *Dream of the Earth*, 11.
6. Ricoeur, "Manifestation and Proclamation."
7. David Abram provides an eco-phenomenological version of this in *Spell of the Sensuous*.
8. Tillich, *Protestant Era*, 112.

and grapes and water to bear the sacred is lost, what becomes of Eucharist and baptism?[9]

Taken together, these critiques suggest a crisis of worship for the Christian community in the midst of climate chaos: both Word and sacrament are in jeopardy. Given that worship is the primary means by which the ecclesia forms its community in a vision of fitting and faithful response to the divine creativity at work in the cosmic process, if worship becomes incoherent, the community is at risk of capitulating to other visions, telling other (less compassionate) stories, and thus can no longer be a force for hope in the midst of diminishment.

Formulating a response to this challenge is a project unto itself, but there are hints of renewal already at work. In 2000, St. Stephen's Lutheran Church in Adelaide, South Australia celebrated a "season of creation" in worship. For four weeks they retold the great creation stories, repented for their role in the impoverishment of creation, and recommitted to participate in the great work of mending the world. This practice spread throughout Australia and to the United States, New Zealand, and other parts of the world. The Season of Creation found its place beside Advent, Christmas, Lent, Easter, and Pentecost. The elements of the earth found their place alongside the elements of bread and wine and water. Liturgies were developed celebrating the wild beauty and the life-sustaining fecundity of oceans, fauna and flora, forests, rivers, wilderness, and storms, often culminating with the practice of blessing the animals on or about the feast day of St. Francis of Assisi. Of course the elements of creation have always been present in Christian worship—the bread and wine and water, but also earth and wood and air that make possible the worship space—but such elements often lie dormant. The Season of Creation helps to awaken us to the constitutive role of such elements in our lives and worship.

There are many other signs of "practicing the new creation." Just looking around the Southeast (my region): The Eco-Stewards Program is a week-long, place-based trip each year that allows young adults to connect their faith with environmental issues. In 2014 the program met in Gainesville, Florida, with the theme Food and Faith: Uniting Together in a Southern Foodshed. The group studied food and water issues in North Central Florida and explored the intersection of faith, community, and agriculture.

---

9. It is important to add that, for Tillich, nature must be brought into the history of salvation in order to be "liberated from its ambiguity." "Its demonic quality must be conquered by the new being in Christ" (ibid., 103).

The 221st General Assembly of the Presbyterian Church (USA) considered an overture calling on the PCUSA to divest from oil, gas, and coal companies. This overture was inspired by the work of Bill McKibben and 350.org in raising consciousness on "global warming's terrifying new math," namely, that the amount of carbon already contained in proven reserves—the amount of carbon we are invested in burning—is five times higher than the maximum amount of carbon (the "carbon budget") scientists say we can burn before risking ruinous and runaway climate change.[10] McKibben argues that it is necessary to weaken the economic and political power of the energy companies in order to give us any hope of keeping all that carbon in the ground and thus preventing catastrophic climate change. Many faith communities in addition to some within the PCUSA are participating in that work.

Georgia Interfaith Power and Light (GIPL), a nonprofit organization committed to mobilizing a religious response to global climate change, is holding a home energy audit training class at the Immaculate Heart of Mary Catholic Church, teaching attendees about energy efficiency and reducing their carbon footprints. At Beall's Hill Community Garden at Centenary Church, GIPL is hosting a feast focused on local and seasonal foods, with conversation on sound farming practices and environmental stewardship.

St. Francis's Episcopal Church in Macon, Georgia, has two large vegetable gardens maintained by their gardening guild, the Merry Gardeners. Compostable materials are used to grow okra, corn, greens, broccoli, squash, tomatoes, and other vegetables that are in turn used to support the congregation's outreach programs.

Oakleaf Mennonite Farm, founded by the Berea Mennonite Church in East Atlanta, is a vegetable and small animal farm that uses organic and ethical practices, affirming that local, fresh, and responsible eating is part of the call to faithful stewardship. They sell their products through a Community Supported Agriculture (CSA) program.

Also known as subscription farming, in a CSA individuals support local food production by partnering with local growers, buying a share of their produce. In this way individuals receive locally grown food and the farmer receives a stable market. It also shares risk and raises consciousness: a local drought now affects the farmer and the consumer. Many congregations participate in CSAs, encouraging their congregants to subscribe,

---

10. See McKibben, "Global Warming's Terrifying New Math."

buying "shares" to provide healthier food for people in need, or serving as pick-up locations.

Food and eating practices are areas of profound religious significance in Christian scripture—dietary laws and contestations around the boundaries for table fellowship are central to the text; it could even be argued that the primal sin of Genesis 2 is "unfaithful eating"—so this is a fitting place for faith communities to reflect on their individual and communal practice.

In these ways and countless others organizations and congregations are "practicing the new creation." These are seeds planted in fertile soil, but we cannot know what they will produce. We cannot know how our participation in the great work of nurturing beauty and life and love will shape the trajectory of the future. We cannot know whether the universe will scatter into the cold and the night or endure forever through some inexplicable eruption of divine creativity. Julian of Norwich trusted that creation would endure because of divine love. Erazim Kohak trusted that all that was good and true and beautiful would be forever inscribed in eternity. We may join with Julian in affirming divine love; we may join with Kohak in affirming the divine creativity that takes up into the deepest possible harmony all the beautiful and broken creatures of the earth. But we must also acknowledge that, while creation itself will endure, our particular trajectories, and the human trajectory, may not endure. We cannot know such things.

But we may have a foretaste of glory divine, we may experience the beauty of the new creation here and now, by contemplating the world as a good in itself, rather than simply as a good for us. True, we cannot do this perfectly; we still need to eat, we still need to use creation. But we may contemplate it in this way haltingly, and we may practice to deepen our capacity for such contemplation. We may go out to meet the beautiful other; we may become beautiful ourselves in so going out; we may be suffused with the divine beauty that both lures forth ever-new, fecund possibilities and gathers up all that has become. Hope for the new creation is hope for creation itself, in all its fragile beauty. It is hope for the dirt, the dirt in which we stand, the dirt of which we are made. In such hope we may not only taste the new creation; we may also learn to cherish and preserve the creation we already have. We may even discover that they are one and the same.

Bibliography

AAAS Climate Science Panel. "What We Know: The Reality, Risks and Response to Climate Change." http://whatweknow.aaas.org/wp-content/uploads/2014/03/AAAS-What-We-Know.pdf.

Abram, David. *The Spell of the Sensuous: Perception and Language in a More-Than-Human World*. New York: Vintage, 1996.

AFP. "Study proves climate a trigger for conflict." http://www.abc.net.au/science/articles/2011/08/25/3302020.htm?site=science&topic=enviro.

Anderson, E. N. *Ecologies of the Heart*. New York: Oxford University Press, 1996.

Armour, Ellen. "Toward an Elemental Theology: A Constructive Proposal." In *Theology That Matters: Ecology, Economy, and God*, edited by Darby Kathleen Ray, 42–57. Minneapolis: Fortress, 2006.

Armstrong, Dave. "Big loss of biodiversity with global warming." http://www.earthtimes.org/climate/big-loss-biodiversity-global-warming/2229/.

Auth, Katie. "Record High for Global Greenhouse Gas Emissions." http://vitalsigns.worldwatch.org/vs-trend/record-high-global-greenhouse-gas-emissions.

Bangert, Byron C. *Consenting to God and Nature: Toward a Theocentric, Naturalistic, Theological Ethics*. Eugene, OR: Pickwick, 2006.

Barr, James. *Biblical Faith and Natural Theology*. Oxford: Clarendon, 1993.

Barth, Karl. *Church Dogmatics*. Edited by Geoffrey W. Bromiley and T. F. Torrance. Edinburgh: T & T Clark, 1956–1974.

———. *The Epistle to the Romans*. Translated by Edwyn C. Hoskyns. Oxford University Press, 1933.

Berry, Thomas. *The Dream of the Earth*. San Francisco: Sierra Club, 1988.

Borenstein, Seth. "UN report dials up humanity's global warming risks; scientist says 'We're all sitting ducks.'" http://www.dailyjournal.net/view/story/f55f61eaf6594e70bebadd360d848640/AS--SCI--Climate-Report/#.Uzwh4KhdWSq.

Brown, Lester R. "Peak Water: What Happens When the Wells Go Dry?" http://blogs.worldbank.org/water/peak-water-what-happens-when-wells-go-dry?cid=EXT_TWBN_D_EXT.

Brown, William P. *The Seven Pillars of Creation: The Bible, Science, and the Ecology of Wonder*. New York: Oxford University Press, 2010.

Brueggemann, Walter. *Theology of the Old Testament*. Minneapolis: Fortress, 1997.

———. *Threat of Life: Sermons on Pain, Power, and Weakness*. Minneapolis: Augsburg, 1996.

Brunner, Emil. *Justice and the Social Order*. Translated by Mary Hottinger. London: Lutterworth, 1945.

BIBLIOGRAPHY

Bryson, Bill. *A Short History of Nearly Everything*. New York: Broadway, 2004.

Calvin, John. *Calvin's Commentaries*. Grand Rapids: Baker, 2005.

———. *Calvin's New Testament Commentaries*. Edited by David W. Torrance and Thomas F. Torrance. Grand Rapids: Eerdmans, 1959–1972.

———. *Institutes of the Christian Religion*. Philadelphia: Westminster, 1960.

Carroll, B. Jill. *The Savage Side: Reclaiming Violent Models of God*. Lanham, MD: Rowman & Littlefield, 2001.

Chesterton, G. K. "Ecclesiastes." In *The Collected Poems of G. K. Chesterton* (New York: Dodd, Mead, and Co., 1911), 310.

Christ, Carol P. "Embodied Thinking: Reflections on Feminist Theological Method." *Journal of Feminist Studies in Religion* 5 (1989) 7–15.

Clements, Ronald E. "Patterns of the Prophetic Canon." In *Canon and Authority: Essays in Old Testament Religion and Theology*, edited by George W. Coats and Burke O. Long, 42–55. Philadelphia: Fortress, 1977.

Climate Vulnerability Report. http://daraint.org/climate-vulnerability-monitor/climate-vulnerability-monitor-2012/findings/.

Curry, Patrick. *Ecological Ethics: An Introduction*. Cambridge: Polity, 2006.

Darwin, Charles. *The Descent of Man, and Selection in Relation to Sex*. Princeton, NJ: Princeton University Press, 1981.

Davaney, Sheila Greeve. "Problems With Feminist Theory: Historicity and the Search for Sure Foundations." In *Embodied Love: Sensuality and Relationship as Feminist Values*, edited by Paula M. Cooey, Sharon A. Farmer, and Mary Ellen Ross, 79–95. San Francisco: Harper & Row, 1987.

Davis, Ellen F. *Scripture, Culture, and Agriculture: An Agrarian Reading of the Bible*. Cambridge: Cambridge University Press, 2009.

Dolan, Eric W. "Belief in biblical end-times stifling climate change action in U.S.: study." http://www.rawstory.com/rs/2013/05/01/belief-in-end-times-stifling-climate-change-action-in-u-s-study/.

Edwards, Jonathan. *The Nature of True Virtue*. Ann Arbor, MI: University of Michigan Press, 1960.

———. *Scientific and Philosophical Writings*. The Works of Jonathan Edwards, vol. 6. New Haven, CT: Yale University Press, 1980.

Eiseley, Loren. *The Immense Journey*. New York: Vintage, 1957.

Farley, Edward. *Divine Empathy: A Theology of God*. Minneapolis: Fortress, 1996.

———. *Faith and Beauty: A Theological Aesthetic*. Burlington, VT: Ashgate, 2001.

———. *Good and Evil: Interpreting a Human Condition*. Minneapolis: Fortress, 1990.

Farley, Wendy. *Tragic Vision and Divine Compassion*. Louisville: Westminster John Knox, 1990.

Francis, Jennifer A., and Stephen J. Vavrus. "Evidence linking Arctic amplification to extreme weather in mid-latitudes." *Geophysical Research Letters* 39 (2012) L06801.

Fretheim, Terrence E. *God and the World in the Old Testament: A Relational Theology of Creation*. Nashville: Abingdon, 2005.

Gatta, John. *Making Nature Sacred: Literature, Religion, and Environment in American from the Puritans to the Present*. New York: Oxford University Press, 2004.

Gilkey, Langdon. *Nature, Reality, and the Sacred: The Nexus of Science and Religion*. Minneapolis: Fortress, 1993.

BIBLIOGRAPHY

Gillis, Justin. "Climate Change Seen Posing Risk to Food Supplies." http://www.nytimes.com/2013/11/02/science/earth/science-panel-warns-of-risks-to-food-supply-from-climate-change.html?_r=1&.

Gupta, S., et al. "Chapter 13: Policies, instruments, and co-operative arrangements." IPCC AR4 WG3 (2007) 747–807.

Haldane, J. B. S. *Possible Worlds and Other Papers*. New York: Harper & Brothers, 1927.

Hargrove, Eugene C. *Foundations of Environmental Ethics*. Denton, TX: Environmental Ethics, 1989.

Hartshorne, Charles. *Born to Sing: An Interpretation and World Survey of Bird Song*. Bloomington, IN: Indiana University Press, 1992.

Hefner, Philip. "The Future as Our Future: A Teilhardian Perspective." In *Hope and the Future of Man*, edited by E. H. Cousins, 15–27. Philadelphia: Fortress, 1972.

———. *The Human Factor: Evolution, Culture, and Religion*. Minneapolis: Fortress, 1993.

Heschel, Abraham J. *The Prophets*. Vol. 1. New York: Harper & Row, 1962.

Jonas, Hans. "The Concept of God after Auschwitz: A Jewish Voice." In *Mortality and Morality: A Search for the Good after Auschwitz*, 131–43. Evanston, IL: Northwestern University Press, 1996.

Julian of Norwich. *Showings*. Mahwah, NJ: Paulist, 1978.

Keller, Catherine. *Face of the Deep: A Theology of Becoming*. London: Routledge, 2003.

———. *From a Broken Web: Separation, Sexism, and Self*. Boston: Beacon, 1986.

Kohak, Erazim. *The Embers and the Stars: A Philosophical Inquiry into the Moral Sense of Nature*. Chicago: University of Chicago Press, 1984.

Laden, Greg. "It's the Heat of the Night." http://scienceblogs.com/gregladen/2012/09/06/its-the-heat-of-the-night/.

Lane, Belden C. *Ravished by Beauty: The Surprising Legacy of Reformed Spirituality*. New York: Oxford University Press, 2011.

Leopold, Aldo. *A Sand County Almanac*. New York: Oxford University Press, 1949.

———. *Round River*. New York: Oxford University Press, 1993.

Levin, Jerome D. *Theories of the Self*. Washington, DC: Hemisphere, 1992.

Lindbeck, George A. *The Nature of Doctrine: Religion and Theology in a Postliberal Age*. Philadelphia: Westminster, 1984.

Luisi, Pier Luigi. *The Emergence of Life: From Chemical Origins to Synthetic Biology*. Cambridge: Cambridge University Press, 2006.

McDaniel, Jay B. *Of God and Pelicans: A Theology of Reverence for Life*. Louisville: Westminster John Knox, 1989.

McDougall, Joy Ann. *Pilgrimage of Love: Moltmann on the Trinity and Christian Life*. New York: Oxford University Press, 2005.

McFague, Sallie. *The Body of God: An Ecological Theology*. Minneapolis: Fortress, 1993.

———. *Life Abundant*. Minneapolis: Fortress, 2000.

———. *Metaphorical Theology: Models of God in Religious Language*. Philadelphia: Fortress, 1982.

———. *Models of God: Theology for an Ecological, Nuclear Age*. Philadelphia: Fortress, 1987.

———. *Super, Natural Christians: How We Should Love Nature*. Minneapolis: Fortress, 1997.

McFarland, Ian A. *Difference and Identity: A Theological Anthropology*. Cleveland: Pilgrim, 2001.

BIBLIOGRAPHY

McKibben, Bill. "Exxon Mobil's response to climate change is consummate arrogance." http://www.theguardian.com/environment/2014/apr/03/exxon-mobil-climate-change-oil-gas-fossil-fuels.

———. "Global Warming's Terrifying New Math." http://www.rollingstone.com/politics/news/global-warmings-terrifying-new-math-20120719.

Met Office. "Met Office 2013 annual global temperature forecast." http://www.metoffice.gov.uk/news/releases/archive/2012/2013-global-forecast.

Moltmann, Jürgen. "Antwort auf die Kritik der Theologie der Hoffnung." In *Diskussion über die "Theologie der Hoffnung" von Jürgen Moltmann*, edited by Wolf-Dieter Marsch, 201–38. Munich: Chr. Kaiser, 1967.

———. *The Coming of God: Christian Eschatology*. Minneapolis: Fortress, 1996.

———. *Ethics of Hope*. Translated by Margaret Kohl. Minneapolis: Fortress, 2012.

———. *Experiences in Theology: Ways and Forms of Christian Theology*. Translated by Margaret Kohl. Minneapolis: Fortress, 2000.

———. *The Future of Creation*. Translated by Margaret Kohl. London: SCM, 1979.

———. *God in Creation: A New Theology of Creation and the Spirit of God*. Translated by Margaret Kohl. Minneapolis: Fortress, 1993.

———. *Man: Christian Anthropology in the Conflicts of the Present*. Translated by J. Sturdy. Philadelphia: Fortress, 1974.

———. "My Theological Career." In *History and the Triune God: Contributions to Trinitarian Theology*, translated by John Bowden, 165–82. New York: Crossroad, 1992.

———. *The Spirit of Life: A Universal Affirmation*. Translated by Margaret Kohl. Minneapolis: Fortress, 1992.

———. *Theology and Joy*. Translated by R. Ulrich. London: SCM, 1973.

———. *Theology of Hope: On the Ground and the Implications of a Christian Eschatology*. Translated by James W. Leitch. Minneapolis: Fortress, 1993.

National Snow & Ice Data Center. "Arctic sea ice extent settles at record seasonal minimum." http://nsidc.org/arcticseaicenews/2012/09/arctic-sea-ice-extent-settles-at-record-seasonal-minimum/.

Nichols, Jordan. "Has climate change created a monster?" http://www.climatesciencewatch.org/2012/10/26/has-climate-change-created-a-monster/.

———. "'Climate of Doubt'—Money Buys Skepticism." http://www.climatesciencewatch.org/2012/10/25/climate-of-doubt-money-buys-skepticism/.

Niebuhr, H. Richard. *The Meaning of Revelation*. Louisville: Westminster John Knox, 2006.

———. "The Only Way Into the Kingdom." In *War As Crucifixion: Essays on Peace, Violence, and 'Just War,'* 15–16. Chicago: Christian Century, 2002.

———. *The Responsible Self: An Essay in Christian Moral Philosophy*. San Francisco: Harper Collins, 1978.

———. "War As Crucifixion." In *War As Crucifixion: Essays on Peace, Violence, and 'Just War,'* 24–29. Chicago: Christian Century, 2002.

———. "War As the Judgment of God." In *War As Crucifixion: Essays on Peace, Violence, and 'Just War,'* 17–23. Chicago: Christian Century, 2002.

Northcott, Michael S. *The Environment and Christian Ethics*. Cambridge: Cambridge University Press, 1996.

Ogden, Schubert M. *The Reality of God and Other Essays*. Dallas: SMU Press, 1977.

Ortner, Shelley. "Is Female to Male as Nature Is to Culture?" In *Making Gender: The Politics and Erotics of Culture*, 21–42. Boston: Beacon, 1996.

BIBLIOGRAPHY

Ottati, Douglas. *Theology for Liberal Protestants: God the Creator.* Grand Rapids: Eerdmans, 2013.
Pascal, Blaise. *Pensées.* London: Penguin, 1966.
Plumer, Brad. "Is Sandy the second-most destructive hurricane ever? Or not even top 10?" http://www.washingtonpost.com/blogs/wonkblog/wp/2012/11/05/is-sandy-the-second-most-destructive-u-s-hurricane-ever-or-not-even-top-10/.
Reynolds, Terence. "Two McFagues: Meaning, Truth, and Justification in *Models of God.*" *Modern Theology* 11:3 (1995) 289–313.
Rice, Doyle. "Report: Climate change could render much of world uninhabitable." http://content.usatoday.com/communities/sciencefair/post/2010/05/report-climate-change-could-render-much-of-world-uninhabitable/1#.UynpUahdWSp.
Ricoeur, Paul. "Manifestation and Proclamation." In *Figuring the Sacred: Religion, Narrative, and Imagination,* 48–67. Minneapolis: Fortress, 1995.
Rizzolatti, Giacomo, and Laila Craighero. "The mirror-neuron system." *Annual Review of Neuroscience* 27 (2004) 169–92.
Rolnick, Philip. *Person, Grace, and God.* Grand Rapids: Eerdmans, 2007.
Rolston III, Holmes. "Disvalues in Nature." *The Monist* 75 (1992) 250–87.
———. "Does Nature Need to Be Redeemed?" *Zygon* 29 (1994) 205–29.
———. *Environmental Ethics: Duties to and Values in the Natural World.* Philadelphia: Temple University Press, 1988.
———. "Kenosis and Nature." In *The Work of Love: Creation as Kenosis,* edited by J. Polkinghorne, 43–65. Grand Rapids: Eerdmans, 2001.
———. "Perpetual Perishing, Perpetual Renewal." *The Northern Review* 28 (2008) 111–23.
———. *Science and Religion: A Critical Survey.* New York: Random House, 1987.
———. *Three Big Bangs: Matter-Energy, Life, Mind.* New York: Columbia University Press, 2010.
Romm, Joe. "Brutal Droughts, Worsened by Global Warming, Threaten Food Production Around the World." http://thinkprogress.org/climate/2012/03/07/381411/brutal-droughts-global-warming-threaten-food-production/.
Ruether, Rosemary Radford. *Sexism and God-Talk: Toward a Feminist Theology.* Boston: Beacon, 1993.
Santmire, Paul. *The Travail of Nature: The Ambiguous Ecological Promise of Christian Theology.* Minneapolis: Fortress, 1985.
Schleiermacher, Friedrich. *The Christian Faith.* Edited by H. R. Mackintosh and J. S. Stewart. Philadelphia: Fortress, 1976.
Schreiner, Susan. *The Theater of His Glory: Nature and the Natural Order in the Thought of John Calvin.* Grand Rapids: Baker, 1995.
Schwöbel, Christoph. "Last Things First? The Century of Eschatology in Retrospect." In *The Future as God's Gift: Explorations in Christian Eschatology,* edited by David Fergusson and Marcel Sarot, 217–41. Edinburgh: T & T Clark, 2005.
Shabad, Rebecca. "Water scarcity escalating due to climate change, report says." http://thehill.com/blogs/e2-wire/e2-wire/193350-water-scarcity-escalating-due-to-climate-change-report-says.
Sideris, Lisa. *Environmental Ethics, Ecological Theology, and Natural Selection.* New York: Columbia University Press, 2003.
———. "Writing Straight with Crooked Lines: Holmes Rolston's Ecological Theology and Theodicy." In *Nature, Value, Duty: Life on Earth with Holmes Rolston III,* edited by

Christopher J. Preston and Wayne Ouderkirk, 77–101. The Netherlands: Springer, 2007.
Sittler, Joseph. *Evocations of Grace: Writings on Ecology, Theology, and Ethics*. Edited by Steven Bouma-Prediger and Peter Bakken. Grand Rapids: Eerdmans, 2000.
Snyder, Gary. "Blue Mountains Constantly Walking." In *The Practice of the Wild*, 104–23. Washington, DC: Shoemaker and Hoard, 1990.
Solnit, Rebecca. "Call climate change what it is: violence." http://www.theguardian.com/commentisfree/2014/apr/07/climate-change-violence-occupy-earth?CMP=twt_fd.
Southgate, Christopher. *The Groaning of Creation: God, Evolution, and the Problem of Evil*. Louisville: Westminster John Knox, 2008.
Suchocki, Marjorie Hewitt. *The End of Evil: Process Eschatology in Historical Context*. Eugene: Wipf and Stock, 1988.
———. *Fall to Violence: Original Sin in Relational Theology*. New York: Continuum, 1994.
Swimme, Brian, and Thomas Berry. *The Universe Story: From the Primordial Flaming Forth to the Ecozoic Era—A Celebration of the Unfolding of the Cosmos*. London: Penguin, 1994.
Tanner, Kathryn. *Christ the Key*. Cambridge: Cambridge University, 2010.
———. *Jesus, Humanity, and the Trinity: A Brief Systematic Theology*. Minneapolis: Fortress, 2001.
Taylor, Bron. *Dark Green Religion: Nature Spirituality and the Planetary Future*. Berkeley, CA: University of California Press, 2009.
Teilhard de Chardin, Pierre. *Building the Earth*. Wilkes-Barre, PA: Dimension, 1965.
———. *The Human Phenomenon: A New Edition and Translation of* Le phénomène humain *by Sarah Appleton-Weber*. Portland, OR: Sussex Academic, 2003.
Terzian, Yervant, and Elizabeth Bilson. *Carl Sagan's Universe*. Cambridge: Cambridge University Press, 1997.
Theissen, Gerd. *Biblical Faith: An Evolutionary Approach*. Philadelphia: Fortress, 1985.
Tillich, Paul. "Kairos." In *The Protestant Era*, 32–51. Chicago: University of Chicago Press, 1948.
———. *The Protestant Era*. Chicago: University of Chicago Press, 1948.
Tobis, Michael. "Grim Trajectories." http://planet3.org/2012/10/25/grim-trajectories/.
University of Tennessee. "Dire drought ahead, may lead to massive tree death." http://www.sciencedaily.com/releases/2012/10/121015111445.htm.
Wallace, Mark I. *Fragments of the Spirit: Nature, Violence, and the Renewal of Creation*. Harrisburg, PA: Trinity International, 2002.
West, James. "Check Out This Shocking Map of California's Drought." http://www.motherjones.com/blue-marble/2014/01/look-shocking-picture-californias-drought.
White, Lynn Townsend Jr. "The Historical Roots of Our Ecologic Crisis." *Science* 155 (1967) 1203–7.
Whitehead, Alfred North. *Adventures of Ideas*. New York: Free Press, 1933.
———. *Process and Reality*. Corrected ed. New York: Free Press, 1978.
World Meteorological Organization. "Press Release No. 965: Greenhouse Gas Concentrations Reach New Record." http://www.wmo.int/pages/mediacentre/press_releases/pr_965_en.html.
———. "Press Release No. 966: 2012: Record Arctic Sea Ice Melt, Multiple Extremes and High Temperatures." http://www.wmo.int/pages/mediacentre/press_releases/pr_966_en.html.
———. "WMO Statement on the status of the global climate in 2013." World Meteorological Organization, 2014.

www.ingramcontent.com/pod-product-compliance
Lightning Source LLC
Chambersburg PA
CBHW020854160426

43192CB00007B/926